T0145707

DIALING FOR

DOLLARS

IN A DIGITAL WORLD

THE ONE STEP SALES PROCESS®

DIALING FOR
DOLLARS
IN A DIGITAL WORLD

THE SECRET ART OF
MAKING MILLIONS
OVER THE PHONE

CHRISTOPHER NOON & MATTHEW NOON

Copyright © 2015 by Christopher Noon & Matthew Noon

All rights reserved. No part of this book may be used or reproduced in any manner whatsoever without prior written consent of the author, except as provided by the United States of America copyright law.

Published by Advantage, Charleston, South Carolina.
Member of Advantage Media Group.

ADVANTAGE is a registered trademark and the Advantage colophon is a trademark of Advantage Media Group, Inc.

Printed in the United States of America.

ISBN: 978-1-59932-520-0
LCCN: 2015937795

Book design by Megan Elger.

This publication is designed to provide accurate and authoritative information in regard to the subject matter covered. It is sold with the understanding that the publisher is not engaged in rendering legal, accounting, or other professional services. If legal advice or other expert assistance is required, the services of a competent professional person should be sought.

Advantage Media Group is proud to be a part of the Tree Neutral® program. Tree Neutral offsets the number of trees consumed in the production and printing of this book by taking proactive steps such as planting trees in direct proportion to the number of trees used to print books. To learn more about Tree Neutral, please visit www.treeneutral.com. To learn more about Advantage's commitment to being a responsible steward of the environment, please visit www.advantagefamily.com/green

Advantage Media Group is a publisher of business, self-improvement, and professional development books and online learning. We help entrepreneurs, business leaders, and professionals share their Stories, Passion, and Knowledge to help others Learn & Grow. Do you have a manuscript or book idea that you would like us to consider for publishing? Please visit advantagefamily.com or call 1.866.775.1696.

This book is dedicated to our loving and supportive Family and Friends, our outstanding team of Noon Company employees and of course to all of our 1000's of loyal customers.

—NOON BROTHERS

Thank you to my loving and patient wife Colleen, my centering force in this world and the love of my life.

—MATTHEW NOON

To my brother, Matthew Noon, who always sees the best in people; he saw a hidden talent within me and gave me the confidence to pursue my entrepreneurial dreams. Everyone should be so lucky to have such a positive force in his or her life. Without Matt, this book would have never been written.

I also would like to dedicate this book to my two beautiful children, Ava and Lyla. They are my two biggest fans and I cherish the unconditional love I receive from my little miracles every day.

And finally, to my dearest love and fiancé, Nicole Buck. I cannot imagine a day without her in my life. She is the most caring, understanding, and selfless person I have ever met. It feels like heaven having her in my life and I am so grateful that I found the girl of my dreams.

—CHRISTOPHER NOON

TABLE OF CONTENTS

FOREWORD

I have had the pleasure of building not only one but two great businesses with my big brother, best friend, and business partner Chris. I say brother first because we are; we're brothers first and business partners second. People have always asked me how we do it. How do you run a business with family? For us, it's never been that difficult. My philosophy has always been to keep your ego out if it and to treat everyone you do business with, whether it be family, partners, clients, team members, or vendors, the same exact way you would want to be treated. It really is that simple.

You read about famous family business partners who get into ugly battles over money, and in the end they would rather ruin the business they put their entire life into, their golden goose, than just put their egos aside and continue to work hard as they always have and build a great business. I realize these types of family feuds run much deeper than how I just generalized them, but we all know the fight doesn't start out being about money. It usually starts with something like what kind of paper clip the corporate office should buy, and then the pure essence of their emotions kicks in.

I will never forget the feeling of gratitude I have for my brother. We both know that neither of us would be where we are now without the other. I guess it just goes back to the way our parents raised us, as good honest people. Those are the values that were instilled in us by our parents, Francesca and Thomas Noon. Chris and I are two of four children, and we have two sisters: Katie and Angela Noon. Growing up, we were all very close, as we are to this day. If asked, all four of us would take a bullet for the other in a second.

The day in college when I called my brother and asked him to come home and help me run and manage my small landscaping business was one of the best days of my life. Others at the time asked me, "What do you need him for? You already got the business off the ground and running." As someone who understands their own strengths and weaknesses, the answer was easy. I knew Chris was a sales genius my entire life, so as an entrepreneur, I was just putting the pieces of the puzzle together. I have always been a team player, and my own ego has never clouded my judgment about what I needed to grow a fabulously large and profitable business. I had the vision to execute an opportunity I saw within a marketplace, and Chris had the business and sales strategy to make it happen.

Chris is unlike any salesman I have ever met. He can sell anything to anyone as long as he believes in it. He has an innate and unique ability to read a sales prospect's mind. It's as if he can psychologically plant himself within the other person's brain. He dials into them by reading their speech patterns and mental language. It's an ability I have witnessed in him over and over, both in business and in the broader landscape of life. I don't think he is even conscious of what he is doing, but I have always said he can sell a snow blower in the summer and lawn mower in the winter. I believe he was simply born with a gift of business street smarts. When Chris sells or negotiates, it's as if everything around him is blocked out. He has a laser sharp focus that allows him to think only about the sale he is about to make or the deal he is about to close. It's as if all other areas of his brain shut down and he goes into "the zone." He dials deeply into the other person's mind and psyche as he mines for his gold, like a master of Jedi mind tricks. I have personally witnessed him sell 20 new lawn care customers in one night in the dead of a New England winter with a foot of snow on the ground.

The most rewarding part of watching Chris sell is the excitement and energy he generates within the salesroom. I truly love to watch his sales team's awe and excitement as they witness my brother in action. And the best part, the part I most truly enjoy, is listening on the phone recording to a new client he just sold. They are just as excited about what they have bought as Chris is to have sold it to them. I am convinced that they aren't even excited about the product or service itself that they bought, although that is great too. I believe they'd have bought anything from him, because they aren't so much buying the product or service as they are buying him. Watching Chris in action selling is like watching a stage performer. There is a beautiful rhythm and craft to it, so it really is like watching an art form.

But unlike many other people, Chris has never wasted his great gift. He leverages it with his extreme work ethic and drive to make the next sale! Being his brother, I might sound biased, but at the end of the day I'm a capitalist, and I only invest in people and capital that are going to increase the value of my business. I am well aware that I could never have built a business nearing $10 million in revenue in fewer than eight years without him and other key people in our company, such as Stephanie Lee, our CFO, and John Guariano, our vice president of operations. Mind you, we did it in a mature industry and one that is not in hyper-growth mode like the tech industries that are going through a bubble right now. Furthermore, we are just in the infancy of our growth strategy, and I am very excited for what is to come in the near future for our business.

Chris is not only a great salesman and negotiator but also a skilled teacher. He has trained hundreds of sales professionals using the sales techniques that he is so passionate about. In turn, they too have enjoyed the success of selling the way he does. He has turned many young people into sales stars by showing them how to sell the way he sells, and this includes me as well. For two years as we were building our second company, I sold on the phones with him. I have always been a reasonably good salesman—as an entrepreneur I have had to be—but cold-calling on the phone is a skill he personally taught me. That changed my life, and I learned something very valuable about selling in the process. Everyone can be a great sales person if they put the effort in and have the desire to be successful at selling. I turned out not just to be a good salesman but a great one, which in turn increased my confidence. Overcoming the fear of rejection on the phone made me fearless in every area of my life because it is such a challenging skill to learn.

As we move Noon Turf Care out of its early start-up stage and into a mature business, I am excited to see where Chris will use his special gift next. His achievements in this industry have created quite a stir and buzz from other company owners. He is now consulting, because of all of the phone calls he gets from business owners around the country, and even the world, who want to learn his selling techniques. Just last week a business owner he consulted for visited him from England. I am so happy to see

Chris start his new consulting venture, Green Light Consulting, as I know it will help enhance the lives of many others.

It gives me great satisfaction to know that I was responsible for getting him into the lawn care industry. Making that call to him to propose going into business changed both of our lives forever. The future is wide open for our company, and every year as we grow in size, quality, and strength we help grow the entire lawn care industry. But what gives me the greatest level of satisfaction is the fact that we grow jobs. Each year, we recruit more and more talented young people and teach them job skills that will last them a lifetime. As we do this, we instill the core values of our company to mold the minds of younger professionals, and in doing so we open many doors for many people. None of this would have been possible without Chris's bold sales innovation. You are about to learn how to build a hugely successful business in just about any industry. The secrets are all laid out in this book, but one must not forget that you can never teach passion, drive, and perseverance—the key ingredients to being successful in anything you do.

—*Matthew Noon*

ONE-STEP SALES

I have been an entrepreneur for most of my 18-year career. The first business I owned was a landscape maintenance and construction company I built with my brother and business partner, Matthew Noon. We grew that business into a $2.5 million firm in six years. We sold the business in 2008, only six years after we started it, so that we could focus our efforts on starting a new Internet business model in the lawn and tree fertilization industry. For those of you who are not familiar with the lawn and landscape industry, it is fragmented—similar to many other industries—and many business owners decide to specialize in just one segment of the industry. This is what we did when we launched Noon Turf Care in 2008. We chose to focus solely on building an organic and chemical lawn service that specialized in the science of lawn care through the application of these products. We went to work on our new company the very same month we sold our full-service landscape company.

The first year was challenging. We had to start a new business from scratch with limited capital and resources. Aside from our head controller and office manager, whom we kept on, the buyer of our landscape construction company hired most of our staff. It was October 2008, and we had to book new business for the following spring—and we had to do it fast. Out of necessity, I started cold-calling for our new business, Noon Turf Care, and personally attracted more than 1,000 new residential clients without meeting one of them in person, as it is traditionally done in our industry. By the end of winter 2009, I had sold three entirely new lawn care routes worth of business. That is when I experienced an epiphany and developed the concept I later named **One-Step Sales**. Due to the fact that we had no money to support an outside sales team to perform traditional face-to-face, on-site lawn estimates, I had to quote and sell new lawn care customers right over the telephone. As Plato once said, "necessity is the mother of invention," and this holds true in our company to this very day. It has turned into the ethos of our company's culture. We had so little time and money to start the new company that I did not even leave my desk in the makeshift office we had set up in a garage, and I sold all of our new customers right over the phone despite their stated prefer-ence for an in-person lawn care quote. This was the moment I realized the power of persuasion, and at the time I did not realize I was changing the way our entire industry sold new business. The average new account value for a customer in our business was $800. So in my first year, I totaled $800,000 of new business with a $25 phone and a one-page sales script. We booked more than 1,000 new lawn care clients that winter, and we didn't yet even have a truck or fertilizer spreader to service these new customers in the approaching spring season as I'd promised. This was one of the most challenging and fulfilling years of my professional career. I cannot think of many years when I have worked that hard. My takeaway from my first year in phone sales was that it is possible to build a profitable company very quickly when you combine a telephone, a phone list, and a persuasive salesman mastering the craft of telleselling.

It was that very winter in 2009 that I learned how to telesell. This small innovation that I created out of necessity, then tinkered with all year, finally clicked and changed my life forever. Little did I know at the time, but my first year of dialing for dollars would create the seed capital to build a company that today is approaching nearly $10 million in revenue with nearly 60 employees. It created life-altering wealth for me and my family, while at the same time thrusting my brother and I into the position of industry leaders. After that first year, we followed the same sales process, except we increased the volume by adding more manpower and more prospects into our phone database. That year we generated another million in revenue. The following years, we duplicated the process and averaged 30 to 50 percent growth for several years to come. Within five years we were a $6 million company, with the acquisition of new sales costing our company only $40 versus the industry average of over $150. We ran lean. We had no outside sales staff, no outside sales vehicle, no added tracking device for that sales vehicle, no estimate forms, no expensive sales presentation literature and folders, and no gas bill for the sales vehicle. We simply possessed a small office with a telephone and a team of very persuasive and persistent sales professionals who shared our vision of growing a great company.

In year three we were at $3.6 million in revenue and netted more than $1 million in earnings before interest, taxes, depreciation, and amortization (EBITDA). This was the type of revenue that had taken many of our industry peers over 20 years to grow.

You get the picture: my One-Step Sales process is inexpensive, and it works. While many sales techniques can grow revenue, they don't always grow the bottom line. My techniques do both, and they epitomize the term *profitable growth*. While many company leaders believe that the hyper-growth of a company comes at the cost of profits, my techniques contradict this and prove that both goals can be achieved simultaneously.

MY STORY

Since I was child I have always had a persuasive personality and entrepreneurial traits that I leveraged at a young age. I remember talking my parents into buying me large packages of candy and gum at those wholesale shopping club stores and then going to school and selling the candy individually to my classmates for a profit. I also remember when I was granted my first paper route how excited I was to get my first "real" job at the age of ten. However when I received my first paycheck at the end of the week I was so disappointed about how little it paid for the effort I put forth. As a kid it was no fun waking up at 5 in the morning to deliver papers for such little pay, so I created a solution. I vividly recall calling the district manager of the newspaper delivery company and asking if I could be assigned a larger route of customers to increase my pay. He told me that it was not possible because there was some internal rule at the company that limited the amount of homes every neighborhood kid could have in their route. So I persuaded my brother and younger sisters to also sign up to become paper route deliverers. By leveraging the help of my three other siblings I amassed a huge volume of routes that I delivered to thus increasing my weekly paycheck. Of course, this also entailed me having to persuade my father to assist in driving me to all the homes because there were too many houses for me to deliver to by foot or bicycle, and of course I did not have my driver's license yet.

Another example of my persuasive sales skills was when I applied for college. I applied to over ten universities so there were a lot of applications to fill out, and of course this included the dreaded essays you would have to write. Since I was juggling my part-time jobs, academics, and athletics I talked my very smart younger sister into filling out all of my applications and writing my essays for me. I have always had the philosophy that delegating your weaknesses to others is the smartest way to work, so this was a natural solution to my challenges at the time.

Admittedly I wasn't the best student in school and in college. I just felt that there were so many other fun and more stimulating places to put my energy towards. Although I love learning I just never took to learning in a traditional academic setting. I just always knew that no matter what my academic outcome was, it would not impact the level of my future professional success. There was even one class in college where I literally showed up six times the entire semester. Rightfully so, I ended up failing that class. I was devastated, but I knew deep down that I deserved the grade. It was my senior year and without a passing grade in this class, I would not be able to graduate. Shortly after I received my shamed F and right before graduation, I picked up the phone and called my professor. Basically, I leveled with him. Reflecting back on this experience, I realize that I was already using my natural sales techniques during that very phone conversation. I was honest and forthright, and I blamed nobody but myself; however, I did explain to him that I was working a part-time job to help pay for my tuition and that I also was playing on the college's Division I soccer team, which was a full-time job in itself.

I asked him if I could take the final exam over and perhaps write one of the papers again. My delivery was authentic; it revealed my state of panic, and it screamed out desperation. I chose my words carefully, and when I finally went in for the close, I said, "Professor Smith, I really need to pass this class to graduate. Would you be willing to grant me this one second chance?" And then, silence. I purposely did not speak first. I just let the dead air between us sit for what felt like an eternity. Then he told me something that I was not expecting. He said, "You know, Noon, I've seen students like you in the past struggle with studies, work, and even sports. I appreciate you being honest with me and not blaming your circumstances on others. I was once a poor bastard like yourself, I'm going to give you a B-, and I hope you learned a lesson with the mistakes you've made."

I was speechless. I was fishing for a D, or a C- at best, and this professor gave me a B- for a class I rarely even showed up for? Now this is something that I am not very proud of, but to be perfectly honest, academics were simply never my strong suit, even when I put 100 percent into them. I did learn a valuable lesson that day—perhaps not the one my professor was hoping I'd learn but a lesson about the real world. It was invaluable. The lesson I learned was that you should never simply accept your fate and the reality of "what is." There is room to move things slightly to your benefit when needed. The hand you have been dealt, or the hand you have drawn yourself, is not always the final hand.

Anyone has the ability to change the outcome of many things in his or her life simply by persuading or influencing the final decision, as I did with my professor. I am not encouraging people to just fast-talk their way out of the problems they have created for themselves; however, sometimes that is necessary. And I am by no means proud of my lack of effort in school. As you read on you will discover how hard a worker I really am when I am committed to something and love doing it. I am not a lazy person when it comes to work or raising a family, but I will admit that there were times when I did not put 100 percent of my effort into academics. Needless to say, growing up, I was a very poor student and rarely paid attention in school.

My father, a self-disciplined baby boomer, was always an excellent student, an officer in the air force and a business executive. He was perplexed as to why my homework grades were so high and my exam results were so poor. He obsessed about his academically struggling son and constantly expressed his concerns to my mother. She would always say to him, "Don't worry, Tom. That kid is going to be a salesman. He already has the skills he needs for life, and he's not going to improve them in algebra class." That's not to say that my mother didn't worry, too, but this is what she told herself to justify all of the Ds and Cs on my report card. Years later, I would find out that I had an undiagnosed learning disability.

When I went into business on my own, starting a lawn care company, people thought I was crazy. Unfortunately, there are many linear-thinking people in the world who believe that the only way one can be successful is by going down a very tradi-tional career path. I will always remember a friend's mother who was very judgmental. Her conventional mindset always made her think that one had to be a doctor, lawyer, or business executive to be successful. She would make snide comments on the phone about other people's less traditional careers. She would talk about how her family had the money to do certain things and how being a contractor, or a small business owner, didn't pay very much. Her husband was a lawyer, so one understood why she thought this way.

Fast forward ten years, the first year of my new lawn care company. I had just learned telesales and was making calls using an old autodialer that I'd gotten on eBay. For those who don't know what an autodialer is, it's exactly what it sounds like. It is used to call phone numbers automatically so that the sales rep can constantly speak to prospects, minimizing the downtime between calls. It is a small piece of equipment that looks like a DVD player and is connected to a phone network—or a computer, for those using an Internet phone, in which case thousands of phone numbers can be uploaded from a computer database.

Only a few of us were making calls, and it was during one of our first weeks, so I still had doubts that we could sell to new sales prospects directly over the phone as a business model. To make matters even more challenging, it was a cold January evening in New England, and more than a foot of snow lay on the ground. My team and I were learning how to use our autodialer, and, at the same time, we were trying to learn how to sell lawn care over the phone—in winter. Needless to say, this was very challenging even for us. As I made one of my cold calls, I heard a familiar voice on the other end of the line. It was my childhood friend's mother, the one with all of the prejudgments on how money should and could be made. I was very surprised to be speaking to her, as I had not dialed her number manually. I immediately broke the ice with her and identified myself, and she sounded happy to hear from me—at least, until I went into my explanation about the company I had started and how I was excited to start my lawn care business.

As our discussion progressed, I began to lose her interest, and I knew she was not interested in buying my services or sincerely wishing me well in my endeavors. As we ended the conversation, she made one last comment, "Well, good luck in your new venture, but you do know, Chris, you will never make a million dollars selling lawn care on the phone." I never forgot that comment. I am persistent by nature, but when I hear people tell me I can't do something because of the dogma they live under, it ignites something within me.

As many of you know, when you venture out on your own, you run into a lot of naysayers. Those are the folks to stay clear of, even if they are family members. I don't think this type of person necessarily wishes you failure but that typically they are projecting their own fears onto you. In many cases, it's also a matter of ignorance. In any event, I try to steer clear of these people, and when I do encounter them, I take their negativism and use it as fuel to propel myself to even greater success. You see, that type of adversity can be leveraged mentally to help you succeed. I look at them as opportunities versus potential failures or setbacks. I bank that negativism for those days when selling is tough and everyone is saying no and hanging up on me. Looking back on it, I had days when I was tempted to call my friend's mother to say, "You were right. I didn't make a million dollars selling lawn care; I made $10 million!" But actually I tend to just use those things as motivation, and when I am successful I let it go and fly below the radar.

In sum, teleselling is one of the most challenging sales methods there is in business. You are putting yourself out there to the world and saying, "Buy me, take me!" The risk of rejection is so high that you can misinterpret it as failure. This is not the case, however. Just like any other craft, such as stand-up comedy, negotiating, or stage performance, if you fail at it, it can break you if you don't fully understand the nature of the learning process. You must view the rejections as part of refining your craft rather than believing that you are inherently bad at it. This is why it is so critical to always maintain a positive mental attitude when starting out. There are so many times on this journey when you will want to give up—as I wanted to many times—but you need to persevere, because when you succeed in selling over the phone it will change you into an even more confident person than you already are in business and in life.

CHAPTER ONE

WHO WILL BENEFIT FROM READING THIS BOOK?

It is important to understand that this is not a "get rich quick and easy" type of book. This is a book about how to combine technology, hard work, and persuasive sales skills in an industry that many would call dead. This book shows you how you can still capitalize on selling on the phone and proves its modern day relevance. I learned that my persuasive skills ultimately meant that I have the ability to sell anything to anyone. I soon learned that these abilities were not limited to literally selling goods and services but were also effective for selling in general and in the broader applications of the skill of persuasion. The skill of selling can carry over into almost anything in life. For example, I use my phone sales skills not only to sell goods and services—although this is my favorite type of sales—but also to sell ideas.

I can sell to just about anyone, but I don't mean this in a calculating, conniving kind of way. I want to make it clear that I can't sell things I don't believe to be good. For example, selling newly recruited and hired employees on why our company is the best to work for is something I believe in. Selling bankers on extending our credit line and partnering with us in taking risk to grow and expand our company—that's something I believe in. But selling with the intention of cheating or hurting someone is something I could never do or even contemplate.

My sales techniques are useful for many day-to-day challenges a person might face. For example, selling a sales clerk on providing a discount on a pair of new shoes. I routinely receive 10 and even 20 percent off just by asking. Hotel accommodation is another example. I persuade front desk clerks to upgrade my room when I travel on business. My family and friends love traveling with me because I routinely get perks or discounts and travel services just by asking for them. I call it asking for the "good guy discount." In other words, there is no real reason for me to receive the discount besides the fact that I'm politely asking for it like a good guy would. My family always chuckles when we arrive at a hotel for a family vacation and we receive a free room upgrade or free drink tickets. My wife will ask, "Why did they give us this, Chris?" And I'll reply, "All you have to do is ask."

Even small things make a difference, as for example when I forget to make a credit card payment while traveling and I'm charged a late fee of $25. I'll simply call my credit card provider and point out how much I love the company's services and how long I have been a customer and then politely ask to have the charge removed—and it always is. I even taught my office manager how to do this when we were first building our business and funds were tight.

Whether you are an executive who needs to sell your next promotion to your boss or a manager who needs to sell a new pay structure to your department, it is crucial to have effective sales skills. Perhaps you're a housewife who needs to sell your children on doing their homework or cleaning their room. If you are involved in politics, did you know that political telemarketing is one of the most effective and cheapest methods of increasing your votes? If you are a traditional salesperson or business owner, maybe what once worked for you to hit your sales goals is no longer working.

In my opinion, no one is ever finished improving his or her sales skills. This is a craft that needs constant refinement, for many different reasons. I am always finding ways to improve this skill, and I find it very rewarding when I tweak one or two things in my pitch to create a breakthrough and a gush of new sales success.

For simplicity's sake, this book is mostly devoted to covering the art of the cold-call sale, but as you will see, you can creatively apply these sales techniques to anything in life, and they are guaranteed to make you a more successful person at whatever it is you do. If you follow the simple steps in this sales system and apply them to your business, you are going to significantly increase your sales volume and the value of your business. If you are a sales rep, you are going to significantly increase your sales commission. I can guarantee you that this book will help you become an overall better sales professional, improve you communication skills, increase your self-confidence in all areas of your life, and help you create and build a better sales system for you and your company.

Throughout my life, my awareness of my strengths and weaknesses has been critical in leveraging my strengths into success. As I matured, I carefully transferred my persuasive skills to my professional career in order to get my first job. Later I would apply those skills to my entrepreneurial start-ups. One skill especially, focus, is imperative for a successful sales professional. You have to make a conscious effort to turn off all the noise when you are selling. Whether the noise comes from personal issues or the distractions of other areas of your business, you need to be able to turn it off and sell.

Success and failure in sales are completely dependent on you and the skills that you develop in yourself. If you are a sales professional, your results speak for themselves; anything outside that is just a distraction. You can find all of the excuses in the world to justify why you had a bad sales week or month, but at the end of the day it all falls back on you, the individual. That's why I love selling and I love managing sales professionals. The proof is in the results, and you need to be able to take full responsibility for your own failure in sales.

CHAPTER TWO

TELESELLING VERSUS TELEMARKETING

I want to thank you for taking the first, very important step in your journey in learning how to become more successful in telephone sales. Before we start, you may have preconceived ethical issues with hard selling or don't believe in creating sales-driven culture that uses outbound calls to make things happen. If that's the case, I hope I can change your perception by the end of this book. This book is the story of how I took a start-up residential lawn care company that was bringing in close to no revenue and built it into a $5 million company in five years. During this journey I also created a sales innovation that I named **One-Step Sales**. As I mentioned earlier in the book, this sales approach has disrupted the entire lawn care industry's way of selling its services. In doing so, I disrupted big national players and captured a large market share that I leveraged into a regional company in 2014. One-Step Sales is a unique process that combines traditional inside telesales with the power of technology—creating an effective process that will make you wildly successful at sales.

By reading this book you have taken the very first step in growing your business by millions of dollars per year. First off, this book is an explicit instructional guide on how to telesell and how to build an effective team to telesell. When I use the word *telesell*, I mean literally to close a sale on the phone without ever meeting the prospect in person. I don't want to confuse this term with *telemarketing*, which can mean the same thing but traditionally refers to lead generation versus literally selling goods and services on the phone.

This is *not* a how-to guide on how to generate "leads" over the phone. In fact, I don't even believe in the term *lead*, and I don't let my sales team use the term. The way my company sells, every single prospect out there with a phone number and a lawn is a "lead." If you follow this simple step-by-step sales process, I guarantee that you will at least double your sales volume, either by new customer acquisition or by increasing the sales volume of your current customer base. No matter what you are selling, you can do so right over the phone, thus eliminating significant overhead for outside sales. My One-Step Sales strategy works, whether it is for lawn care, pest control, cleaning services, cars, or any kind of widget. At the very least, it can close your sales loop, making it a much tighter and cohesive process. As a result, you will save time, money, and loss of sales due to competitors beating you to the punch.

I also want to make it clear that in explaining my telesales system—which is effective in organizations of any size—I will focus on the small business owner and the start-up stage, as this was my own experience and because typically this is the most challenging stage of building a business. As many experts and academics have shown, the first five years are the riskiest for a new business venture. My system can dramatically increase a business's chance of surviving the first five years of operation, as it did for my company. I will use many examples from my own experience in taking a stagnant residential lawn care business with revenues of $500,000 per year and growing it to $5 million in five years. If you are like me and seek the ultimate truth and are skeptical of get-rich-quick schemes, you will be relieved to find that there are no magic tricks in this book. The content in this book will teach you how to build a rapidly growing and successful business through the techniques that I have crafted and refined during the early stages of my company. I want you to be successful, as I am, and I wrote this book so that others will have a road map of the process that took me many years to discover and build.

If you are running a much larger organization than what I have just described, I want to be clear that I have seen the techniques of my system applied successfully to companies that enjoy revenues of $10 million and even $1 billion. I guarantee that these sales techniques will help companies of any size if they make the investment. I know this because I have consulted with much larger companies than my own and taught them how to apply my phone sales model to their own businesses, and they have done so successfully.

This book will cover everything you have ever wanted to know about how telesales can help you become more successful at this art. And I mean it when I say "art." I sincerely believe that telesales has much in common with acting, singing, and any other art form out there. I will cover all of the technical aspects of telesales and teach you how to set up an inside telesales department. Finally,

I will teach you how to couple telesales with the Internet and any other form of marketing. Although telesales works brilliantly as an independent sales approach, it can be an even more lethal weapon against your competitor if it is incorporated into a broader marketing campaign such as the Internet, mail, radio, or referrals.

For those just starting out or bootstrapping a new business, telesales is one of the most cost-effective methods you can use. You can apply the One-Step Sales approach that I innovated to any sales campaign. This sales system eliminates the added waste of layers of sales professionals and the added time it takes to sell certain services traditionally, not to mention the frustration of remotely managing outside sales professionals.

The reason I wrote this book is that I was once in your shoes. Starting out in business, you have limited capital to invest in consulting and other business luxuries. In fact, most start-ups that are not funded have only enough money to sign an office lease, with a little left over to turn the lights on. That is the way I began my career. There was no rich uncle at my disposal to lend me money, and I'm sure that is the case for many of you reading this book. Instead, I was forced to become innovative in my quest to be successful in sales. I bootstrapped my own training guide by building the road as I moved along. After creating and refining the One-Step Sales concept, I decided to write this book not only to document my journey and to use it for training within my company but also to share it with others. I did this so that people do not have to invest years of research and experience into learning these lessons—so that they can instead spend their time making new sales on the phone and building their businesses.

As I progressed in learning telesales, I often wondered whether anyone out there had written a concise guide on the subject. I found a big variety of telemarketing services and books, but nothing came close to what I was looking for. Nothing was unique to my industry. I vowed that after years of refining this concept with technology, sales scripts, and recruiting, I would document the process not only for my own records but also to help others avoid this long path. I want to make it clear: this is not a typical how-to-get-rich-quick formula. It is much more difficult than that. You will need to put forth hard work, dedication, and perseverance. Much as I don't want to use the old cliché, it really is all about hard work.

The concepts in this book will give you an incredible edge and save you a lot of wasted time and aggravation in troubleshooting. One of the fundamental rules of success in telesales is that you truly have to be committed to the concept in its entirety or it will not work. Selling over the phone is very challenging, and building a team of professionals that can do it for you is even more challenging. I have spent the past three years consulting in my industry and other industries, and my techniques and strategies have transformed my clients' communication skills, their businesses, and ultimately their lives. After three days of training under my tutelage, they have returned to their businesses and increased their sales by more than a million dollars in revenue per year in many instances.

A few attended my sales camp looking for a way to get rich quick. They were looking to have others put in the hard work for them. I can honestly say that those folks have all failed. Many didn't even make it to the third day. I can recall one lawn care company owner from Texas who visited with a few of his salespeople. Joe was looking for a quick fix to the sales woes and challenges at his company. By day two, he was already defeated when I told him that in order to make his sales team successful, he too had to be committed to it. He had spent money to attend my camp, and rather than spending the precious hours he had with me to learn my concepts, he spent the time trying to poke holes in my sales model. He was a "glass half empty" type of guy, an attitude that—you could tell—rotted right down to his employees as well.

It was very disappointing when the time came for him to get on the phone and close his first cold-call sale. He appeared flustered and a bit shaky. I was sensitive to this because cold-calling is always hard for anyone starting out, including myself. I told him, "It's time for you to get on the phone, Joe." He turned white in front of his sales team and absolutely refused to get on the phone, even after all of the training I had put in, telling him that the owners and managers needed to learn this craft even if they were not going to be the ones calling and selling. Even after all of those hours I had spent emphasizing that to be successful it is important to truly understand what you are managing, he still refused to get on the phone. Sadly, I had to send Joe packing back to Texas with $5,000 less in his pocket and nothing to show for it. Not only did Joe's refusal to get on the phone and dial for dollars let his own team down, but he let me down as well. I hate to see people quit before they even try, because that first phone call could have been the one that built their confidence and transformed them into a great salesman and sales manager. You may ask yourself why I cared so much for him to master this art. I was still getting paid by him, wasn't I? My answer to that is that what I teach usually pays a much higher reward to me than just money. I want to have the satisfaction of showing others that what I teach works, which then reinforces my true belief in telesales. I want people who give me their hard-earned money to learn something that I have to teach, to be successful because they invested in me. I want them to reap the benefits and rewards they will get if they succeed. After all, they are my next referral, my next disciple who will spread the word of the success that my teachings and concepts bring to their company. But one thing I cannot teach is desire. Burning desire to be successful has to come from within. I learned that early on in my own business, when I was building my team—literally. I knew by the first day of training if a new sales professional was going to be successful.

INFORMATION IS POWER

Since I started my lawn care company, we have sold into seven new markets and regions in New England. Starting from scratch in a new market can be very challenging, but if you master cold-calling, it can greatly increase your chances of being successful. It truly puts your finger on the pulse of a new market. When you cold-call a new area, you are able to immediately gather information about that market. You are able to quickly gain information on competitors and their pricing in that area. This will help you structure your value proposition and pricing for your business.

Many times I have simply used my competitors' pricing to splash into a new market. This has saved my company time and money by creating a base of clients and capturing a fast market share. Once we have that, we start to price our services according to our own company's price structure. It is my firm belief that temporarily undercutting competitors when entering a new market on the telephone saves your company a lot of time and aggravation. I am not advising you to be the scab of your industry, but if it is a carefully thought out, short-term strategy to get up and running in a new market area, it works quite well.

For example, while we were entering the Connecticut market last year, we would contact new prospects and see if they were using one of our local competitors. If they were, we would offer to charge them less than what they were currently paying, to motivate them to try our service. This gave us the leverage to capture an initial market share since we had no brand recognition in that area. As ours was an out-of-town company, this strategy minimized any risk our prospects envisioned from switching to a service provider they had never heard of. After that initial sales offer, it was our company's job to build trust by delivering a superior service and product.

LEVERAGING THE TELEPHONE

All successful people have used their unique abilities and talents to self-start. In most cases, all entrepreneurs and salespeople have used some form of leverage to propel themselves to the next level. Leverage is the fundamental component behind any successful enterprise, and I am a big proponent of leveraging anything and everything you can.

A little about my business background is appropriate here. I started my business career on Madison Avenue in New York City, working for a large, national advertising firm. After graduating from college with a degree in business and communications, I went straight to New York to find my fortune. As a naïve graduate in the late 1990s, I figured this would be an easy challenge to overcome in a short period of time. After all, I was raised on 1980s movies in which countless young people were seduced by the glamour of New York City. Soon after arriving, they would find their fortune and live happily ever after.

Within 18 months, as a young account executive scraping by on a starting salary of $30,000, I became disillusioned. When I looked up the corporate ladder, I saw hundreds of older account executives and managers only earning double what I was earning. I knew that even if I did successfully climb this ladder, I would still be unsatisfied with the financial reward when I was promoted. Additionally, the work itself was already beginning to feel very unrewarding. It was during this time that I realized there wasn't anything inherently wrong with the job in general but that it was just not right for me. I was beginning to feel this entrepreneurial drive that I knew I always possessed, even when I was a kid. As I grew older I was always hustling up some kind of side income like mowing lawns in my neighborhood where I grew up or selling T-shirts at rock concerts in college.

My impatient personality needed something faster paced with quicker results and rewards. It was at this time that I began to examine my strengths and weaknesses. I knew I wasn't a company man, and I knew I didn't just want to be a manager. I needed something where I could use my sales skills and feed my desire to be creative. I concluded that the most appropriate next move would be a career in sales and business where I had independence and the opportunity to build my own future without the constraints of an upper management position.

It was during this time that my brother, Matt, called me from Boston. He was attending Boston College and was approaching his final year. He was also running a small lawn mowing business that he had started in high school. He had a problem. The business had grown too big for him to manage while he was trying to finish his senior year thesis. He asked me if I would take it over for a couple of years until he graduated, and in return, he would pay me a lot more money than I was already making. Naturally, since he is my younger brother I immediately turned him down, but my brother is very persuasive—I guess it runs in the family. To make a long story short, he agreed to sell me half of the business, and we became 50-50 business partners.

The business was only a few years old, and somehow my brother had managed to grow it to revenues of more than $400,000, which came as a bit of a shock to me. While I was slaving away in New York for peanuts, he was cutting grass and earning nearly six figures per year in cash! Looking back on this event, if you had told me in college that I would make millions of dollars selling lawn care on the phone, I would have called you crazy. It's funny how things work out. When my brother and I partnered up, we knew that we would quickly need to double the size of the business in order to make it worthwhile for both of us. We quickly split the tasks: he managed the operations and finance side of things, and I managed the sales and marketing side. Our job roles are much the same 15 years later as our business nears $10 million in revenue.

Six years after I went into business with Matt, we had revenues of more than $2.5 million. We offered a full array of services for landscape maintenance, construction, and irrigation. We'd built a highly profitable small business by using direct mail, door knocking, and referrals for growth. In those early days, prior to the sophistication of today's Internet, we also prepriced targeted neighborhoods with a list of the services we offered. This was hugely successful because it was a call to action. Pricing was already included in the direct mail piece, which eliminated the added step of sending a sales rep to the property to price it out.

The problem was not a lack of sales but the ability to effectively execute the completion of the scheduled work.

As I continued to grow my sales team and sales department, the operations could not keep up. We constantly had to scale down work and growth. It became very difficult to grow our business because of the added expenses of labor, administration, and materials required to maintain the growth. Although there are a few companies that have grown their full-service landscape business revenues into multimillions and even billions of dollars, that kind of growth was something we did not want to undertake. By the end of 2007, we were operating a $2.5 million business with a fleet of 20 trucks and a skilled team of about 45 employees. In 2008, we made the decision to sell the company and start over with a new business that did not have the scalability challenges. The landscape business was a great business at the level we were running it. It taught me a lot about how to run a very difficult business, and we made a lot of money doing it, but our hearts weren't really in it. So at the end of the day, we decided to move on.

We chose another outdoor service because we were familiar with it and comfortable in the service industry. We chose to launch a fertilization service for lawns, trees, and shrubs. This business was much easier to grow and sell into, and as it grew naturally, the overhead remained fixed, allowing profits to increase dramatically. Starting over again raised a lot of challenges as well as opportunities.

We now had very little income and support, so we had to learn how to run a lean business again, and we had to give ourselves a very large pay cut. We created a new business plan and now had a very clear vision of what we wanted to build. The challenge was in going from zero revenue to $1 million as fast as we could so that we would be able to start building a customer base and equity again. The opportunity centered on the fact that we were now experts in the service business and no longer wet behind the ears. We started to think strategically for the long term rather than the short term. We calculated that we would need about 1,500 new customers in order to hit the $1 million mark, and we wanted to do it in 12 months.

In fact, we had to do it in 12 months so that we would not drive ourselves into debt. As I look back on this challenge today, it now seems like a crazy thing to try to do without any money for marketing and sales. However, when you find yourself in that situation, and scarcity is looking you square in the eye, you are forced to truly put your mind to it, and you don't think or see much beyond that immediate challenge. You simply begin to survive and adapt by working hard and being as innovative as possible. Although many ventures today are started with seed capital and other traditional investment vehicles, there is something to be said for the entrepreneurs who bootstrap their ventures.

Although starting a business without much capital can be a truly challenging and agonizing process, it is my belief that it is the only way to build a company without losing control. Not having large amounts of borrowed cash to fall back on creates core strength within the company, as it is forced to respond quickly to matters of necessity and treat all else as unnecessary business luxuries. It also means there are only two sets of people to see to: the employees and the customers. This creates a company that takes care of its employees, who in turn take care of the largest asset: the customer.

$5 MILLION IN FIVE YEARS

Working with this mindset, we saw acquiring new customers as the largest challenge for our new fertilization business. Unlike the business model of our previous landscape company, which serviced a small volume of customers at premium pricing, our new business model was servicing a large volume of customers at competitive pricing. Since residential lawn technicians can perform services for more than 25 customers per day, it was necessary to have the large volume in order to create *route density* for our lawn technicians. *Route density* means less "windshield time," which is how our industry refers to downtime. When a lawn technician spends time driving his truck, he is not fertilizing lawns and billing out revenue. It doesn't take a rocket scientist to know that this is waste, and waste equals loss in business.

The more clients you can service on a street or in a neighborhood, the more revenue you can produce per day. In order to do this, you need to acquire customers for the lowest cost possible and do so as fast as you can. As we started to apply similar marketing techniques from our old company to our new business, we came to a very quick realization: direct mail, radio ads, and other means of expensive marketing that had worked for us in the past were not so successful in targeting customers for our new turf care business. Unlike a landscaping service, in which you can make up for expensive marketing campaigns by selling a few premiere landscape projects for $30,000 to $40,000, you need to sell services to a few hundred new fertilization customers for $500 to $600 dollars per customer. In the early days of building our first landscaping business, we burned through considerable amounts of cash as we distributed large direct mail pieces and ran radio advertising campaigns with very little impact. They just did not make our phone ring.

Fast-forward six years, we hit the same wall in our lawn care company during the first year. We quickly realized that no matter how much we marketed our services, we were unable to effectively close a large volume of sales. We quickly did the math on the back of an envelope and found it would take us 20 years to build a $5 million company. We did not like that timing. Although traditional marketing campaigns are effective in building long-term awareness and penetration, we did not have the luxury of time or money. It was clear that we needed a new marketing and sales plan, and we needed it fast.

As I did my research, I came to the realization that the only cost-effective way to quickly kick-start a base of new customers is to telesell. The next five years were a blur for us, but they were some of the most exciting years of my life. The first year we implemented our telesales strategy, it changed the way we did business, and we were able to build an entire business model out of it. During those first eight months of implementing our cold-call plan, I dialed until my fingers bled, as they say. After I had mastered the craft of selling on the phone, I could not stop. It became so natural to me that I was selling seven new customers per night on the phone and as many as 20 when I was really on a roll. Within 12 months, I had sold more than 1,000 new customers!

I considered that first year our breakthrough year, and after that it was simply a matter of putting the pieces together to duplicate and multiply the process. From there, we leveraged a base of customers and revenue that we quickly reinvested in the company. We then built a telemarketing sales team and phone technology that enabled us to acquire new customers at $50 per new sale, down from $150. This substantially increased our profit margins, thus enabling us to reinvest in overhead and future growth. The rest is history. From 2008 to 2013 we grew Noon Turf Care from $250,000 to $6 million. We grew revenues by an average of $1 million per year, and we grew our client base from 300 customers to 8,000. We have a staff of more than 50 employees and a fleet of 40 service vehicles. Today, we close more than $3 million of new company sales via telemarketing.

After our first year of fast growth, we did expand our marketing budget beyond just telesales. I will return to this point in further detail later. Telemarketing works, even with the advent of the Do-Not-Call (DNC) Implementation Act of 2003. In fact, we started our business well past the date when DNC was made a law, so we never knew life before the law. This might be why we were so successful with telemarketing. I am told by colleagues who tele-marketed in the 1980s and 1990s that the level of access to sales prospects' telephone numbers was quadruple what it is today. The way I view that is, if four times the number of prospects existed then without national regulation, probably 100 more companies were calling your sales prospects.

Today, post-DNC, there are still an abundance of sales prospects just waiting to be called. Since only a handful of for-profit companies and nonprofits cold-call today, that leaves very lonely prospects just waiting for their phone to ring and for a friendly salesman on the other side to sell them a product or service that will save them money or fill a need.

THE DIRTY WORD: TELEMARKETING

Telemarketing is the process of using the telephone to generate leads, make sales, or gather marketing information. Unfortunately, the word *telemarket* has a negative connotation and stigma due to a large trend in the 1980s and 1990s in which some companies implemented aggressive campaigns and many times used bait and switch tactics. Consumers were driven crazy by the dozens of telemarketing calls they would receive during dinnertime and evening hours by sales reps pitching the latest, greatest deal of the week. Many of these salespeople were not trained properly and were propped up in front of phones by large corporations to sell better phone plans or mortgage rates.

Telemarketing's origins are believed to date to the 1950s, to DialAmerica Marketing, Inc., which was reported to be the first company dedicated to telephone sales and services. By the 1970s, telemarketing was a common phrase used to describe the process of selling over the telephone. It often included both outbound and inbound calls but later became much more synonymous with the outbound calling we're all familiar with: high-volume, outbound sales calls made by hundreds of people in a boiler room or call center.

By the late 1990s and early 2000s, *inside sales* was the term used to differentiate telemarketing from *outside sales,* the traditional face-to-face sales model in which salespeople went to the client's business or residence to deliver their messages, their sales pitches. By 2004, the list of available phone numbers began to dry up, so many companies chose to diversify and expand their outside sales force.

Telemarketing can be a particularly valuable tool for small businesses in that it offers many of the same benefits as personal selling, but saves time and money. In fact, experts have estimated that closing a sale through telemarketing usually costs less than a fifth of what it would cost to send a salesperson to make a sale in person. Though telemarketing is more expensive than direct mail, it also tends to be more efficient in closing sales and thus provides a greater yield on the marketing dollar.

The American Telemarketing Association found that spending on telemarketing activities increased from $1 billion to $60 billion between 1981 and 1991. By the mid-1990s, telemarketing accounted for more than $450 billion in annual sales. This increased use of telemarketing resulted in an unexpectedly strong backlash. For telemarketing firms, the landscape in the early 21st century changed dramatically. However, as the 2000s has progressed into the 2010s, telemarketing has proven to be alive and well for many companies. With regard to business-to-business sales, not much has changed legally. Thousands of companies around the country continue to thrive in generating sales or, at the very least, warm leads via the telephone.

THE MAN IN THE GREY FLANNEL SUIT: IT'S NOT YOUR FATHER'S SALES JOB

I will always remember when my high school English class read *Death of a Salesman*. I was not much of a student in school, but for some reason I really connected with that book. Perhaps it was my subconscious screaming at me, "When you are salesmen, you will not let this happen to you!" Basically, the story addresses the ever-changing world in business and, more broadly, in life—right up until your death. The protagonist, Willy Loman, is coming to grips with the fact that he can no longer drive and be a successful salesman. Thus sets in the reality of his losing his professional abilities. In one scene, as he speaks to imaginary people, it becomes clear to his sons that his job may not be the only thing he is at risk of losing. He is also coming to grips with the reality that perhaps he never was a good salesman, and, in the twilight of his life, he grapples with what he has accomplished and whether all the work he put into sales and raising a family was justified.

As I matured and read the play again, I realized that the theme runs a lot deeper than that. The story resonated with me and obviously millions of other people, because it is so easy for us, the audience, and the other characters in the play, to judge Willy. After all, it's easier to judge others than it is to truly see our own flaws and shortcomings. Most importantly, it is difficult to come to grips with our own limitations and, of course, mortality.

Willy has to address all of these issues in the play, and in today's ever-changing and often disruptive business climate, sales professionals, like Willy, must face the prospect of their professional abilities becoming insufficient for the increasing challenge of face-to-face selling. We now confront increased expenses, competition, and an educated consumer base. As business overhead and expenses increase, it forces an entire generation of sales professionals to be quicker and more innovative than ever before. Take fuel costs alone. They are enough reason for salespeople to stop selling face-to-face, toss their car keys on their desk, pick up that telephone, and begin dialing for dollars. At the very least, they should be doing this to screen their sales prospects and to arrange a meeting with them if what they sell requires it.

I find it amazing that many sales professionals scour the streets looking for business, on foot and in their cars. I see it happening on a daily basis at my office: salespeople wander into our office, offering to save us money on office supplies or equipment parts, and they tirelessly try to get past the best gatekeeper in the business: my executive assistant. It just seems like such an inefficient and costly way to grow a business.

I'D RATHER HAVE A ROOT CANAL

When I was a child, our family phone would ring incessantly during the dinner and evening hours. My father was a very traditional family man, and dinnertime was considered sacred. When the phone rang during these hours, my father would become infuriated to the point that he would throw the receiver off the hook, and then that obnoxious off-the-hook buzz would start. It was an evening ritual that became almost ceremonial, indicating that it was "dinnertime." My mother and siblings and I would awkwardly stare down at our plates, trying not to laugh in my father's presence, trying not to laugh at the absurdity of the entire thing. I would always wonder why he didn't just turn the ringer off during dinnertime or even unplug the phone from the jack altogether.

On other nights when the phone would ring, my mother could not ignore it. You could see her eyes light up as the ring seduced her. (Those were the days before caller ID.) She'd be hoping her sister or a friend was calling. On some nights, to my father's dismay, she simply could not resist, and she would pick up the phone. It never seemed to bother her when, instead of a relative or friend, it turned out to be a Bell Atlantic saleswoman from Delaware who wanted to save her money on her phone bill. My mother, to this day, simply loves chatting on the telephone.

Outside of dinnertime, my father would answer the phone, when he was in a good mood, and chat away politely to the telemarketer on the other end of the line. Some days, to everyone's surprise, he would even buy whatever the telemarketer was selling. He often smiled when he hung up the phone and bragged about how he had just saved $5 a month on our phone bill. On other days, when he was not in such a good mood, he would pick up the phone and scream at the poor person on the other end of the line because he was just not in the mood to talk.

One evening my father hung up the phone after purchasing a new phone subscription package and said, "That phone solicitor was actually a nice woman, but gosh, I'd rather have a root canal than do what she does for a living." For some reason the phrase "root canal" always stuck with me. It was years before I even learned what a root canal was, when I got one myself—and then I really knew what my father was talking about.

As a kid at evening dinner times like these, I realized the power of the phone. The experience also taught me that people are only human, that when you call to solicit them you need them to be in the right mood—a buying mood, that is. This helped me early on in my telesales career, because I did not take it so hard when someone answered the phone and screamed at me. It also taught me to keep a positive mental attitude when I was dialing, because I simply needed to find the right person in the right mood. This mindset made dialing more of a numbers game than an exercise in formulating the perfect pitch or hitting a home run every time I made a sales call.

MENTORSHIP

I think one of the most important keys to success in anything is to seek out a mentor. I wish I had learned this earlier in my career, as it would have prevented me from making a lot of unnecessary mistakes and given me the ability to build a vision for myself by learning how somebody older and more experienced had found success. If you are young and in business: find a good mentor. After making the decision to telesell when we were starting out, I knew that I would need some training and guidance on the subject. I knew that the largest and most successful lawn care companies in the country had built their business with phone sales, but I still did not have the first clue about how to implement this strategy.

When I reached out to find training support, I was shocked at how little was out there. I realized that I would have to get creative in finding my own help. Luckily, through some industry contacts, I found TC, a sales manager from Tulsa, Oklahoma who was known as the Oracle of Okie. He was a telemarketing legend from the 1980s and 1990s who had sold thousands of customers and built dozens of lawn care and pest control branches for many of the large national companies.

Once I located him, I called him out of the blue and asked if he would teach me how to sell on the phone. At the time, he was managing a telemarketing sales department for a Scotts franchise owner in Michigan. He was so good at telemarketing and managing a sales team that the Scotts franchise owner agreed to let him call out of Tulsa to his prospects in Michigan so that he did not have to relocate with his wife to Michigan. At this point, he was semi-retired after more than 20 years of dialing for dollars. I owe my education in telesales to TC, who, to this day, is a great friend.

He agreed to teach me. In fact, he told me that if I flew down to Tulsa he would make me a telesales success in four days. Mind you, aside from selling for my company with warm leads and inbound sales inquiries, I had zero experience in outbound cold-calling. I eagerly took him up on the offer, and my brother and I flew down to Tulsa to learn the art of the phone. Before we booked our flights, TC gave me two references to call. They were other lawn care company owners who had also taken his training course. I was excited to talk shop with these fellow lawn care operators from other areas of the country. I expected them to gush about how TC had made them overnight millionaires and how they had mastered the craft of telesales. However, this was not the case when I spoke with them.

One of them recommended that I try a different sales approach. Surprised by this suggestion, I asked him if TC's training was helpful. He said it had been very helpful, but it was just too hard to find phone numbers anymore with the advent of DNC. When I asked the second reference about TC's training, he also spoke highly of him but said when he returned home he decided against launching a telesales department. When I asked him why that was, he said, "I'd rather eat spiders." I laughed at this response but also realized that not everyone is cut out for teleselling.

Looking back on our success, I can't even imagine building a company without using the phone. After all, face-to-face sales create slow sales growth and unnecessary sales overhead. I've also come to learn that company leaders would rather not tell the truth about why they don't telesell; they would rather just say they do not believe in the practice and that it does not fit into their culture or blame it on an external force such as DNC laws. In my opinion, they can't handle the blow to their self-image that comes with telling themselves, "I can't do this." The fact of the matter is, they are too scared to do it, and they psych themselves out before they even give it a chance. Why sales reps or business owners limit their company's success because of fear is beyond me. They only hurt themselves and their company. As in many cases in life, these types of naysayers are simply projecting their own fears of teleselling onto others when they say that telesales does not generate quality sales with which to build a quality book of business. This is simply not true. For example, the majority of my sales for my lawn care company are sold on the phone, and our account value per client is double that of the national competitors. Meaning, we also charge a premium for our services because our product is better than many of the other competitors in our market. Lastly, our client retention rate is also well above the industry's benchmark, which means these customers sold over the phone not only buy premium service, but they are loyal, too!

My point is that telesales is not as hard or as scary as people claim. Most of the people who are against it are just scared. It's not that they have an ethical issue with it. With that in mind, I am a bit relieved that other lawn care companies in our market don't do it, because it provides more opportunity and a competitive advantage for us. In business, I will take any leg up on the competition that I can get. Rather than listen to others, I am one who tends to draw my own conclusions.

My telesales mentor, TC, was a very friendly and intense older gentleman. He had the lines in his face and gray in his hair of someone who has spent the majority of his career phone selling, and judging by his intense and upbeat attitude, I would bet the majority of his phone selling career was spent cold-calling. As I mentioned earlier, cold-calling is the hardest of the hardest. As TC would tell me constantly, "You have to have a positive mental attitude, always, when selling." He had many one-liners like that and was well aware of the need to create a positive and upbeat work environment.

TC taught me how beautifully simple telesales is as a sales system. There is no need for fancy brochures, elaborate sales campaigns, or even expensive company sales vehicles. As I mentioned earlier, all you really need is a telephone and a marketing list. TC also showed me the importance of keeping your overhead low when you start selling on the phone. His sales office was located in a small, rundown strip mall outside the city. Inside was a modest training room and a break room with a coffee maker brewing some grocery store coffee.

In the back office was the sales room. It was a traditional-looking "boiler room" with about eight sales reps feverishly cold-calling prospects. Every 10 or 15 minutes a sales rep would get up from his chair and announce that he had closed a new sale, and everyone would cheer. Then he would walk to the front of the room and mark a point on a chart, indicating his new sale. Within seconds, people would be back on the phones, riding off the energy of the recent sale and hoping they were next in line. What I witnessed was incredible. Who would have figured that you can sell lawn care this way? It was the middle of January, but the energy of the room felt like a busy lawn care office in May. These guys were months ahead of the demand curve because they were looking for clients rather than waiting until spring when the clients would be looking for them. It all came together for me. It was Sun Tzu's *Art of War*. You need to beat out your competitors before the season even begins.

Four days of training with TC in Tulsa changed my life. I am glad I didn't listen to the biases and preconceived notions of others. It also taught me a valuable lesson: to always research my findings independently. TC gave me the foundation for how to sell on the phone, how to build successful telemarketing campaigns, and how to build a team to telemarket. Once I made my first sale on the phone in Tulsa the first day I was there, I was a believer—I was hooked on telesales. Returning to Boston, I quickly set up shop at our office, organizing a telesales system of my own. I will delve deeper into this later.

My point is, once I mastered the art of the sale on the phone, and learned for myself by actually getting on the phone and doing it, I was sold on the concept. You can't manage something or invest in something that you are not familiar with. So before you begin to even think of building your own sales room with a team of sales professionals, you must try it for yourself. You need to walk the talk. You need to learn telesales one step at a time, and after that, things begin to fall into place.

The following 12 months were still not easy. It took a lot of time and hard work to craft my pitch and refine my closes, but it worked. I would dial from morning until night, and with every new sale that I closed, my self-confidence would increase. This self-confidence would compound and build on itself, and slowly but surely I mastered the art. As a musician masters an instrument and an actor masters a character, I too attained mastery. I mastered the art of the cold call and closed one sale after another.

THE THREE TYPES OF SALES REPS

In my 15 years of sales experience, I have trained some of the best salespeople in my industry. I have never subscribed to the idea of "natural born" salespeople. On the contrary, I do not listen when people say, "I'm not a salesmen," or "I could never sell for a living." The fact of the matter is, we have all sold in some fashion or another in our lifetime. You might have sold your point in a conversation, sold something you enjoy to others (such as a hobby or favorite type of food), or sold your personality, character, or even your good looks when you met new friends. You have also probably sold your apology when asking for forgiveness after you made a mistake. In fact, we are always selling. So you can understand why such claims of "being" or "not being" something drive me crazy. Of course, just like anything else, you might not enjoy doing something, but that does not mean you are unable to do it. With that in mind, I have found that sales professionals fall into three different categories. They could be categories that sales professionals have placed themselves in, or they could be categories their company has created for its employees.

1. **Order Takers:** I liken Order Takers to the classic Maytag Man. That classic image of an appliance repairman shows someone sitting in his shirt and tie, staring at the phone, and waiting for it to ring. This person knows all about the product, and he knows all about the company. He has all of the answers and seems to be right for the job of selling. There is one thing, though: he *cannot sell*. Order Takers cannot call themselves salespeople. They don't have the *attitude, desire, or work habits.*

2. **Salespeople:** These people are better than Order Takers. They can work independently, have some drive and work ethic, and make a decent living, but that's where it ends. Salespeople have a goal each day, week, and month. At the end of each day, if the goal is reached, they stop and go home—that is, it could be noon, 5 p.m., or 9 p.m., but when Salespeople achieve the prescribed number of sales, they quit.

3. **Master Closers:** They are the best. Master Closers operate on a different level from that of the Order Takers and Salespeople. They listen, learn, understand, and use a lot of charm and wit to solve problems simply and directly. Master Closers can think faster and better than the customer and their mediocre colleagues. It's all

about showmanship. They use all of the resources to sell their service the way actors use props. They are always selling, convincing, driving, and always winning. They are sold on their products and service. Master Closers will always meet goals and then keep on going to exceed them. In the sports world, they call it "running up the score." This occurs when a team continues to play with the goal of increasing its points even after the outcome of the game is no longer in question and the team is assured of winning. Bill Belichick and the New England Patriots are well known for this. One of the biggest blowouts he led was in 2009 when the Patriots beat the Titans 59–0. It went on record as the second biggest blowout, right behind the 1940 game when the Chicago Bears beat the Washington Redskins 73–0. Belichick claims he does this out of respect for the game and the opponents, because he believes there is always a chance for an opposing team's comeback. I think the team members also do this in order to challenge themselves as a team. Why not compete against yourself once you have beaten the competition? Some judge it as a classless display of arrogance and dominance, but I view it as good sportsmanship. Master Closers do the same in the game of sales. I always tell my team this, because as most salespeople know, they will be starting again at zero the next day. If you are in the zone, this type of sales momentum builds off itself, and you become unstoppable when you are on a sales roll. It's almost as if each new prospect on the phone can sense your earlier success and confidence and become more likely to buy from a winner than a loser. They seem to almost have a subconscious desire not to let you down. Your positive energy of success is pure, and they do not want to get in the way of your aligning stars, so they buy what you are selling.

CHAPTER THREE

OUTBOUND COLD-CALLING: GETTING STARTED

When you begin your cold-calling campaign, it is important to first create a neat and organized working space. It sounds like a small and petty issue to address, but good housekeeping is essential. As I tell my team, "a clear work space creates a clear mind." Make sure your desk and computer is clear of anything not related to your sales task at hand. This means eliminating distractions from your desk such as additional paperwork, personal items (including your cell phone), and any other items not related to sales. You may laugh, but I go so far as to make my team check in their cell phones at their supervisor's desk to help them resist the temptation of answering personal phone calls or text messages.

A couple of years ago, personal cell phone use among my employees got so bad that I bought one of those cell phone "jails" from Amazon. It was more to make a point than anything else. This cute little contraption looked like a mini-prison equipped with individual cells, where I could lock up the phones until it was time to take a break. It caused a mutiny at first, but over time productivity went up, and I was even thanked by one employee for sparing him the distraction of constant text messages from his wife about all of her daily trivial activities.

You also should close any programs and documents on your computer monitor. I liken being behind a computer on sales calls to flying a helicopter. Cold-calling requires a sales professional's undivided attention at all times. One small distraction can cause you to crash and burn. After all, you don't see a helicopter pilot texting and flying at the same time. The only items open on your computer should be your sales/company software and, in our case, mapping software for measuring prospects' lawn sizes. The only items sitting on your desk should be your sales scripts, product and service information, a closing script, a calculator, and a pad and pencil to jot down notes. I will be revisiting the software tools and scripts later.

THE DO-NOT-CALL REGISTRY (DNC)

One of my most successful turnarounds with a sales prospect occurred just six months after I started. I made a sales call to the neighbor of one of my new customers as I realized the importance of route density for the profitability of my company. When I cold-called my existing customer's neighbor, the neighbor was not happy, to say the very least. She proceeded to scream at me in colorful language about how she was on the DNC list and how she was going to call the attorney general. I calmly and politely apologized to her and stated that I did not know she was on the DNC list. I proceeded to tell her that all of the phone numbers I buy are supposed to be filtered and devoid of people on this list.

After I calmed her down, she apologized for reacting the way that she had.

I then mentioned to her that I owned a local lawn service that fertilized the lawn of her neighbor, who was really happy with the results. She apologized again, because she was close friends with her neighbor. At that point, I was in the clear. I went into a friendly sales pitch about how I would love to deliver the same results for her lawn and said I would give her a discount for causing her any inconvenience. She ended up buying my service, and six years later she is still a client. I always refer to this story when I am training new sales people to teach them a valuable lesson.

I teach them that they need to remain calm in situations like this and remember that we are just local professionals checking to see if other people in the neighborhood are interested in what we have to offer. Overreacting to people's emotions causes a domino effect that never ends well. Some people just tend to react emotionally, and it is the sales professional's job to take control of the situation by calmly diffusing things. It is our job as sales professionals to keep an even keel and to remain in control of the conversation. Doing so calms the other person as you carefully lead the conversation to a positive outcome. The same holds true for any similar situation in service.

In my industry, there are two types of lawn care companies—the ones that believe in sales and marketing as an integral part of building a successful business, and the ones that do not. Lawn care operations and customer service are obviously very important in running a successful business, but in order to have the appropriate client volume to be profitable, you need to sell. The implementation of DNC in 2004 changed the landscape of the entire telemarketing industry. The DNC list has made cold-calling residential prospects very challenging for large and small business owners in this country. It has also created a lot of preconceived notions about telemarketing in general. For example, some business owners think it is simply illegal to cold-call. This is not true, and in the past six years my company has legally sold millions of dollars of new business right on the telephone. I would like to clear up some of the misconceptions by stating the facts regarding DNC:

1. The National Do-Not-Call Registry gives you a choice about whether to receive telemarketing calls at home.

2. If homeowners choose to be on this list, they must register their information with the National Do-Not-Call Registry.

3. Telemarketers should not call a homeowner's number once it has been on the registry for 31 days.

4. If homeowners registered on this list are called by a prospecting company, they can file a complaint on the DNC website: www.donotcall.gov.

5. Homeowners can also verify that they are registered by checking this site.

6. Homeowners may still receive calls from companies with which they have an existing business relationship for up to 18 months after their last purchase, payment, or delivery from the company unless they specifically ask the company not to call again.

When you purchase phone numbers and prospect lists, it is important to verify that your lists have been scrubbed clean of names and numbers that are registered with the Do-Not-Call

Registry. The marketing company that provides you with the list will also be vigilant in scrubbing these numbers, because it can be fined for violating the DNC law by selling data that has not been cleansed. In summary, I look at the DNC situation as an opportunity, not as a hindrance, in growing my company. It never ceases to amaze me how some lawn and pest business owners simply eliminate outbound phone sales as an option for growing their businesses, using DNC as their excuse. In my humble opinion, they are either too lazy or too scared to pick up the phone and cold-call. Just because there are now laws that protect the consumer does not mean that it is illegal or unethical to cold-call. Just as in any industry, businesses simply need to be aware of the laws and follow them in order to protect their interests.

SMILING WHILE DIALING

I believe anyone in business can be successful through natural talents and, of course, hard work. Another huge factor is attitude. At our company we call it PMA, a Positive Mental Attitude. The motivational speaker and businessman Zig Ziglar has a very famous quote that I love: "Your attitude, not your aptitude, will determine your altitude." It is important when you are making cold calls that you are seated upright at your desk and that you are always smiling. People can actually hear you slouching when you speak on the phone to them. More importantly, they can hear you when you smile. Customer service experts urge any phone professional to "smile when you dial." It is even more important to have a positive attitude, because you are in the business of convincing others to buy what you have to sell. No one wants to buy something from someone who has a bad attitude—it just does not feel good.

Remember, you are cold-calling prospects to deliver good news about how your product or service is going to have a positive impact on their life. Bad attitudes are simply not tolerated in my salesroom—or anywhere in my company, for that matter. Bad attitudes can spread like cancer, and they can begin to erode the entire fabric of your company. With that in mind, you must make a conscious effort to stay positive even after a lot of rejection on the phone. Cold-calling is not for everyone. You certainly need thick skin for it. Making a conscious effort to stay positive and let the rejection roll off your back is critical to succeeding in sales, especially when you are cold-calling.

WARMING UP

One of my top salespeople, Jeffrey C., has been in the phone sales industry for years, and he has his own routine to warm up in the morning before dialing. Similar to a baseball pitcher practicing his pitching in the bull pen, Jeffrey practices his phone skills before getting on the phone for his shift. Each day, he stops by my office, which is located right by our sales department, to make small talk. He always has his first cup of coffee in his hand, and he is smiling ear to ear. He tells me what he did over the weekend, asks about my family, and things like that—small talk. Like clockwork, after about ten minutes, he shifts to discussing how business is and how excited he is about our new lawn care sales offer. He tells me how excited he is for the spring to come, even when it is January and there is a foot of snow on the ground.

When Jeffrey started doing this, I took it in stride. It was not until months later that it dawned on me that there is a reason Jeffrey does this—discussing our company's great offerings and positive attributes, which I already know about—every day without fail. At a certain point, I realized he was using me to warm-up before getting on the phones. It was his way of rehearsing his lines, warming his vocal chords up, and—most importantly—energizing his positive attitude.

If you haven't seen the movie *The Pursuit of Happyness*, starring Will Smith, I strongly recommend that you watch it. The movie came out during a period when I had my first child, purchased a new home, and started the business I have today. As they say, when it rains, it pours. I distinctly remember that stressful period of my life and all of the risk associated with the things I just referred to. Would I be able to provide for my family? Would I be able to make my mortgage payments? Would my new business venture survive the first five years? I am a strong proponent of risk taking. Risk pushes us to achieve greatness, and you need this force in your life to motivate you and challenge you to reach your full potential.

The movie, based on a true story, depicts Chris Gardner, a single father who is temporarily homeless and struggling to break into a career as a financial advisor. Gardner did not have an easy upbringing, as he never knew his biological father and was abused by his stepfather. In the film, Gardner is scraping by, just trying to survive as a commission-only stockbroker. To make things even more challenging, he is one of the only African American salesmen in the company he works for and has very little training or education in finance. His rags-to-riches story is truly inspiring, and I was glad I watched the movie when I did, because I thought, "If he can do it, I can do it." Gardner works his way up within the financial company by cold-calling prospects to set up sales meetings in person. He has to maximize his time on the phone because he is a single father who can put in only six hours of selling, rather than the nine hours his colleagues are logging. The story has a remarkable ending as Gardner goes from a homeless person to one of the most successful stockbrokers in the country.

Today he has multiple financial service firms, is a best-selling author, and runs a media company. Chris Gardner exemplifies the American dream and is a prime example of what hard work, perseverance, and a positive outlook on life can do for the future of you and your family. My main point in highlighting this story is what Chris Gardner credits with leveraging his success and future: the telephone and hard work. Below is a scene from the film in which Chris explains how he got his break in cold-calling. Chris dialed his way out of poverty and went on to become a wealthy and successful man.

> *Whoever brought in the most money after six months was usually hired. We were all working our way up call sheets to sign clients. From the bottom to the top. From the doorman to the CEO. They'd stay 'til seven, but I had Christopher. I had to do in six hours what they would do in nine. In order not to waste any time, I wasn't hanging up the phone in between calls. I realized by not hanging up the phone, I gained another eight minutes a day. I also wasn't drinking any water, so I wasn't wasting any time in the bathroom.*

It was during this scene that Chris finally connects with a very wealthy CEO who gives him his first shot by buying stock from him. The reason I emphasize this scene is that when you are first starting out, the only thing coming between you and success is a telephone. The more disciplined you are and the harder you work, the more successful you will become. It is truly that simple, too. You need to properly manage your time and stay focused. Remember, cold-calling is a numbers game: the more calls you make, the more you will sell.

Here are three key takeaways from the clip:

1. **Stop wasting time:** Salespeople can waste a lot of time researching prospects before a cold call. You don't need to know as much as you think when you are calling to pitch a prospect. All you need to know is the name of the person and what your service costs. That's it. There is a reason why our call center agents can crank out more than 180 calls per day for our enterprise customers.

2. **Find ways to be more efficient:** Scarcity breeds innovation. You will surprise yourself with all the ways you think of to become more efficient when you have to.

3. **Ask for the sale:** There's only one way to find out if people will buy from you. You need to ask them! I will return to this point later in the book.

SALES SCHEDULE

Time is money! Old sayings like this stick because they're true. Every one of the successful salespeople I have met in my career has a strict schedule they always adhere to. Since the very first day I sold on the phone, I have had a very strict schedule for myself, and I strongly recommend this to everyone. As my mother used to say when we were kids, everyone operates better on a schedule. You want to set up your schedule around the optimal time your prospects will be answering the phone. For business-to-business sales, this will most likely be traditional business hours: from 8 a.m. to 5 p.m. For business-to-consumer sales, these hours will vary, depending on what you are selling and which time of year you are selling, but they should generally be within the prime-time hours of early afternoon to evening.

Again, with my residential lawn care company, we are targeting suburban homeowners with lawns, people who typically work a nine-to-five job. Sometimes, one of the spouses will stay at home raising the children, and we will be able to connect with that person during the afternoon hours. So we call from noon to 8 p.m., and we take short, 15-minute breaks every two hours. We also take a longer 30-minute break around 6 p.m. so that we can eat our dinner and get right back on the phones for prime-time selling hours. At the height of our selling season, which is late winter/early spring, we also work Saturdays from 9 a.m. to 2 p.m. when homeowners are usually home, as the weather isn't that great and they are not yet outside on weekends doing yard work or shuttling their children to sports activities and other events.

Most experienced salespeople can make 250 to 350 cold calls per shift. From my experience, I am convinced that anyone can be successful if they are committed to calling consistently. I always tell my new hires that it's all numbers. The more calls you make, the more likely you are going to get a sale. It's not necessarily about overcoming a rejection. It's about finding that one prospect who is going to say yes to what you are selling before you even call. It's similar to fishing. The more times you cast your line out there, the more likely you are to catch that fish. I would rather have an average salesperson who works hard and consistently makes calls than an above-average salesperson who does not have a great work ethic and makes fewer cold calls. On average, my sales team will make one sale every 75 calls. That is an average of four new sales per day and 20 new sales per week. The more you call, the more you sell. That's the bottom line.

THE IMPORTANCE OF GOALS

In college I played soccer for Seton Hall University's Division I team. Growing up, I was always a very good soccer player, and my skill really improved by high school. I was one of the best defenders in the league in high school, but I never imagined I would one day play for a Division I college team. I was always grateful for the way my parents pushed me to reach my full potential as a player. They saw the talent I possessed even before I did. I can't tell you how many practices and games they schlepped me to as a kid, since I played for two different teams.

When I was growing up, my father would stress how important it was for me to set goals for myself. By high school, my athletic goal was to play soccer for a Division I college. I did everything I needed to do to create exposure for myself to college soccer recruiters. I played on the private soccer club teams, I played on the state team, I went to elite summer camps, and I trained on my own for hours at a time in school vacations and in the off-season. I went to dozens of college recruiting camps. When my senior year in high school approached, I still had not been contacted as a recruit. I began to set my expectations lower and to focus on playing for a Division II or a Division III school, but my parents encouraged me not to give up on my original goal to play for a Division I school. I guess you could say that I was unable to see the forest for the trees. So I pursued my goal, applied to Seton Hall University, and was admitted.

There was still no guarantee that I would make the college's soccer team, and I had to walk on and try out. The rule in the NCAA is that college sports teams are required to have tryouts open to all students who were not recruited to the team preseason. The tryouts are basically considered a joke among coaches and players, as they rarely ever find a "hidden talent" among the hundreds of walk-ons. In fact, when I tried out, the soccer team had already been practicing as a team for more than a month prior to the start of the season. There is a very small chance of being selected for a spot on a team as a walk-on, but I stuck to my goal and gave it my all. It was a two-hour tryout with more than 300 walk-ons gunning to make the roster.

When the selections were made, I ended up being the only player out of all the participants at the tryout to make the team. Even today I am astonished to think back on the odds that I beat in making the team. It was because I followed my goal all the way through to the end. I went on to be one of the top defenders in the league, scoring 13 penalty kicks. This taught me a valuable lesson in life: set your goals and set them high. Even if you don't always hit the goal, you can come somewhere close to it. As in my soccer career, you will surprise yourself by achieving a goal that you didn't even think was possible when you set it.

Setting Goals 12 Months per Year

I always loved the grade school story about the grasshopper and the ant. Maybe that's the simple man in me, always valuing the virtues of hard work. The story is one of Aesop's Fables and a moral lesson about the virtues of hard work and planning for the future. It tells of the difference between the ant and the grasshopper. The grasshopper spends its time singing and playing all spring and summer while the ant spends its time working and stocking food for the winter. When winter approaches, the grasshopper is starving and looking for food, he knocks on the door of the ant's home, which is secure, warm, and well supplied.

To work today is to eat tomorrow. That is the message of the story and has always been my philosophy in business. In most cases, it has to be, or the business will fail. When applied to our company's sales strategy, it hits the nail on the head because we are a seasonal business. If we don't have our ducks in a row by spring, we will have missed the seasonal demand and can never earn back those months of lost sales. The moral of my story is that you should sell all year round, whether in peak season or the slowest season. Every sale counts.

I still apply the lessons in goal setting that I learned from my soccer experience to the businesses I run. When I started out selling all by myself, my business coach recommended that I write down my initial sales goal for the year. When I wrote it down, he told me to add 30 percent, which I reluctantly agreed to do. I had a calendar for each month of the year and marked each day with my specific sales goal. Back then I was trying to sell five new sales units per day, six days a week, with Sundays off. I held myself accountable to these numbers for the entire week and month without exception. If I failed to hit my goal of five units and only sold four, I adjusted my goal to six units for the following day. That year, I actually beat my goal and went on to sell more than 1,000 new customers, which was the sweat equity we needed to get off the ground. By writing these very specific goals down on a daily basis, I was held accountable for my goals. If, by that Saturday, I had not achieved my goal, I would stay until I had, even if it required making calls into the evening.

Today not much has changed besides the fact that we now have more than 20 salespeople held to this very same standard. Every October, my executive team lays out our company goals for the following year. I make them write out these goals on paper so that they are recorded and visible, virtually set in stone. We write down goals for sales, profitability, and growth, and we discuss them on a quarterly, monthly, and even daily basis. Sales goals are discussed daily so that we remain committed to them and never lose focus.

When you first write down sales goals for yourself, it can be scary. You are consciously documenting a goal you are not 100 percent sure you can hit. Your entire company strategizes operations based on hitting that goal. When you lay out your annual sales goal, it is important to not make the goal too low or too high. You don't want to defeat yourself or your team with goals that are too high, and you don't want low goals to cheat you out of additional sales you could have pushed for.

After you create your sales goal for the year, you want to break it down by month, week, and day. You also want to take into consideration your sales cycles, adjusting goals according to when high and low demands occur, for whatever you are selling. For example, our lawn care company's peak sales season is January to May, so goals are set higher in these months than in the summer season, when demand slows down.

When you create goals, it is also important to create one metric to use in managing them. This will depend on the type of service or product you are selling. You can use number of units sold, number of clients sold, or total amount of revenue sold. We use units at our company, but there is no right or wrong metric to use, as long as you use only one and you use it consistently.

It is then important, in managing your own goals and the goals of others, to display the results in your sales room where they are visible to everyone. Laying out the week and then tallying the progress toward the goal—basically keeping tabs on our team members' sales results—enables us to stay on track every single day. It also helps create a competitive environment for our team. Sales professionals are naturally competitive, so when they see someone beating them on the sales board, they want to catch up, not only for higher commission checks but also as a matter of pride in leading the room. The only way to create this atmosphere of competition is to display goals and progress openly. Once upon a time, we simply used a dry erase board, but now that we have grown and need to be as efficient as possible, our goals and progress are displayed on a digital screen. The data is entered in a computer by our sales manager.

It is important to make sales not something to fear but something to be inspired by. For example, if you begin to hit your goals consistently, you should slowly raise the bar each month. Compete against your own past success and keep pushing yourself. There is nothing more rewarding than ringing up the sales board when you are on a roll, as Bill Belichick does in football. Ringing it up is essential if you want to be a great closer. Just as I described earlier, you always want to go above and beyond what your goal is, given the opportunity. This is what sets a great salesperson apart from a good salesperson. If you achieve your goal early in your sales day, use the excitement and confidence of having a great day and go above and beyond, leveraging the adrenaline high you are on.

Prospects will sense this when you are on the phone with them—it is infectious. Ringing it up is a must. After all, you never know what tomorrow will bring. It is also important that when you do achieve these goals, you celebrate. Celebrating success is essential in creating inspiration for the following week, not to mention a great way to blow off some steam. When my sales team hits record sales goals, I buy pizza for the whole room at the end of the week, and I also hand out cash or gift cards to top producers. We also have monthly and annual fixed bonuses that are much higher. For example, we will pay one large additional payout to the sale rep at the end of the year if they hit their total annual sales goal in addition to their monthly and weekly goals. Whether or not they hit their annual goal, we walk them through their sales results for the entire year. We do this so that the sales professional is aware of the total impact he or she has on the company's overall success for the entire year. Combining short-term (weekly) and long-term (annual) sales goals allows the sales rep to see through both sets of lenses. When you do this it prevents the sales rep from giving up or losing hope if they miss their sales goal for a week or even a month. They know that it is never too late to catch up, because if they don't receive their weekly or monthly sales bonus they can still receive their annual bonus if they work their butt off for the remaining months or even weeks of the year; they still have skin in the game.

It is important to dangle that carrot for yourself or, if you are a manager, for your team. Money is not the only thing that can drive a sales rep or a sales team. To motivate some teams and to boost the morale of a sales group you can also create little celebrations as a team. I remember one sales season that was so successful I took my team of ten reps and rented a room at the Capital Grille one Friday evening, and we celebrated our success by ordering anything we wanted on the menu, including bottles of champagne. These recognitions of success go a long way in inspiring sales team members to achieve the best results they can.

I will leave you with one more example of someone who has attributed the majority of their success to goal setting and hard work. I do this because goal setting and persistence, in my opinion, are the most important characteristics one needs to be successful in cold-calling. They are more important than any other talent or skill a person may possess. The person I am referring to is Kathy Delaney-Smith, head coach of women's basketball at Harvard University and arguably the most successful Ivy League coach in history. She has had the most wins of any Ivy League women's basketball coach, and she owns a 31-year coaching record of 495–340 at Harvard with a 295–127 record in Ivy League play.

She has coached eight Ivy League Players of the Year, including three-time winner Allison Feaster ('98) and two-time recipient Hana Peljto ('04). She has also coached six Ivy League Rookies of the Year and 36 first-team All-Ivy League selections. She has coached all 18 members of Harvard's 1,000-point club. Finally, she even worked through the year that she was diagnosed and treated for breast cancer, the 1999–2000 season.

Needless to say, her coaching record is very impressive, as well as inspiring. When interviewed by 90.9 WBUR, she was asked about her unusually long tenure in coaching one team. She said, "Probably the single thing is that I have stayed at Harvard for 32 years because I passionately and deeply believe in, educationally, what women's basketball is as part of an undergraduate degree."

Jessica Gelman, who is one of Delaney-Smith's former athletes and students, says this about her former coach, "Her saying is 'act as if,' which, basically, is when you feel terrible, when you're sick, when you're tired, act as if you aren't. There are going to be days when you just don't feel as good as you would like, but you've got to act as if. And I think she preached that to us when we were all 18–22, and that was really setting the ground stone for who we are and what we believe in today."

This is exactly the attitude you need in the sport of cold-calling. I have already referred to this, but I think it is necessary to highlight it again because it is so critical to success in sales in general. Perseverance is so important. On many days, you will just not feel 100 percent. Those are the days that you need to dig in and work through, just like an athlete. The reason is that if you stick with your goals and continue to make those calls, the next person who answers the phone will most likely say yes, and once you close that sale, you will be back on top both psychologically and professionally. You need to always remember to "act as if" the next call you make is going to be your next sale. Again, cold-calling is purely a numbers game, a fact that can be proven mathematically. The more calls you make, the more sales you make.

CHAPTER FOUR

VALUE PROPOSITION

Once you have committed to cold-calling and telesales, it is important to develop your sales systems and tools so that you can focus while dialing for dollars without distraction. I will first address outbound cold-calling because it is the most primal form of selling and one that delivers the greatest results. Cold-calling requires no upfront marketing costs, and, unlike many types of order taking that occur in sales, you are proactively making the phone ring rather than sitting around and waiting for it to ring. As I always tell my sales professionals and consulting clients, that phone isn't going to dial itself.

First off, it's imperative that you fully understand the product or service that you are trying to sell on the phone. There is nothing more jarring than listening to salespeople stammer and stutter as they attempt to make their sales pitch before they are familiar with the product or service. It's like watching an actor forget his lines in a play or a newscaster misreading his teleprompter on television. It's absolutely painful to hear.

Remember, you are contacting prospects out of the blue to convince them to buy something that, in most cases, they didn't even think they needed seconds before your phone call. In most cases, you will be peppered with questions by the prospect, so it's best to be as prepared as you can be. This means understanding the entire value proposition of your product or service. A value proposition is a promise of value to be delivered and the customers' belief that they will experience value. Basically, you must answer the question of why your product is better. Are you selling on price, quality, or a combination of both? What makes your product better or different? Can you schedule faster than the competition? What are your terms for payment?

My lawn care company's value proposition is that we are a privately owned company with local and personal service, unlike the national chains. We apply golf-course grade products and offer a free, 24-hour turnaround should there be any issues with your lawn between services. You are also assigned the same lawn technician for the entire season to create personal and consistent service. There are no binding contracts, and you can pay for service as you go throughout the season. Because you are giving us this opportunity to care for your lawn, we are also going to provide you with a complimentary lime application this season. Should you decide to prepay or sign up for autopay, you would receive an additional 10 percent service discount. Of course, our value proposition goes much deeper than that, but this is our basic sales pitch, and, oftentimes, it just takes this for a prospect to agree to use your service.

This may sound elementary, but for outbound cold-calling, your value proposition is critical because the prospect always has the upper hand. You need to be able to communicate quickly and concisely why the prospect needs your product or service without losing the prospect's interest or having the phone hung up on you. It always helps to have a special promotion, particularly with cold-calling. Promotions or discounts are not always needed if you have a superior product or service, but in cold-calling, I believe they are essential to grabbing prospects' attention. Remember, you are simply calling them to deliver this news to them and to make this promotion available to them, as a good friend or neighbor would. So knowing your product or service is essential, and the more you know it and can answer questions about it, the more professional you will appear to be. You want to remember that professionalism builds trust, and trust sells.

In terms of vocabulary, when you are cold-calling, it is important to remember that words are your most valuable asset. In fact, words and the vocabulary you use are your only assets, and they must be utilized wisely. I read an article about Jerry Seinfeld, a comedian who acted in, arguably, the most popular sitcom in history. The interviewer asked him his secret of success as a stage comic and why he became so successful while other comedians fell short in comparison. His answer was simple: in order to stay sharp in his craft he had to stay active on the stage. He explained that stage comedy is like a muscle, and if you don't keep it active and fit, it loses its strength. Seinfeld's answer to this question resonates so deeply with me because telesales is the exact same way. Whether you are on stage as a comic busting chops or on the phone as a salesperson dialing for dollars and closing sales, the act of honing your craft is very similar—you need to stay active!

PHONE GREETING

When you are making more than 300 cold calls, you will be talking to a wide variety of people who answer the phone. For residential prospects, the daytime hours are the most challenging because most decision makers are not home. I still find it important to call during those hours, though, because you are likely to make at least one or two sales before the power hours of 4 p.m. to 8 p.m. This also allows you some time to warm up for the important hours when you truly need to be running on all cylinders. Most of the people who answer the phone at this time of day are housewives, nannies, elderly people, parents of the homeowners, and even cleaners—I have never understood why house cleaners answer the phone, especially when they don't know English. Toward the late afternoon you will start to connect with the more qualified buyers, usually the husband or wife. It is important to keep in mind that not everyone who answers the phone is going to be excited that you called. You may have interrupted your prospects when they were in the middle of doing something, or they may have been speaking to someone on the other line. It's imperative to always be respectful of prospects, even when they don't reciprocate. It is important to remember that you are their virtual guest and that you can stay only if they allow it.

I have heard it all when cold-calling. People have screamed at me, threatened me, called me not-so-nice names, and, of course, hung up on me. Always avoid contention and stand on higher ground if people become combative. If they have specific questions about how you got their name and number, just tell them the truth and apologize for bothering them. I think people behave differently on the phone than in person. On the phone, they often have less patience and forget their social graces and manners. Perhaps it's because they can't see you, and they feel you have intruded upon them. Whatever the case may be, it's important to always use your best phone etiquette and imagine that you are knocking on their door.

I have cold-called in dozens of markets around the country, and I know for a fact that people will buy goods and services over the phone in any market. However, it is important to recognize the subtle differences in each market, and you need to intimately understand the social behaviors of people in your calling market. Of course, you are not calling Mars, and there aren't huge differences, but you need to recognize that there are differences. For example, my company calls into the New England market. New Englanders are, typically, tough on the exterior and not very warm people. Who knows? Perhaps it's their Puritanical roots. Regardless, you need to be prepared for this type of personality. They are usually well-educated consumers and environmentally conscious, so you need to truly understand what you are selling because they are going to pepper you with educated questions. What I enjoy about the New England market is that once you are in, you are in. Yankees are very loyal consumers once you build trust with them.

Some of the Midwest markets, on the other hand, are very friendly and open. I was surprised by this when I was undergoing cold-call training in the early 2000s. We were calling Ohio and Michigan, and the prospects would always thank us for calling and wish us luck with the rest of our sales calls. They came across as being more casual than New Englanders. This is not to say that midwesterners are uneducated, of course, or pushovers as consumers. They were just a lot warmer on the phone, which I liked. From my recollection, they were also more focused on the service and results than on environmental concerns or customization of their lawn care program. They just wanted to know the price, the guarantee of results, and when we would be starting.

Every region and market in the country is different, so I urge you to truly understand your market and potential consumer before starting a cold-calling campaign. It really helps to know the little cultural nuances and differences of each calling market. You need to be aware of the small cultural differences in each market so that you can adjust your selling style to meet that of the market you are calling.

Now, no matter what market you are calling in, people are people. Catch them on a bad day, and they might bite. It's important not to react emotionally to prospects who greet you on the phone with angry and colorful language. You need to remind yourself that you caught them on a bad day and move on to the next call. I also want to mention that it is still possible to close these types of folks once you have calmed them down. The good news is that you will also be greeted by some very nice and cordial people, and those are the ones you want to put your energy into selling once you have qualified them.

The evening hours are prime time, and most people have more time to talk on the phone at night. Additionally, they are usually more relaxed, as they have been home for a while and have had some time to unwind. During the prime-time hours, the likelihood of closing sales increases significantly. We refer to the final hour of selling for the evening—typically at 8 or 9 p.m., depending on the market—as the power hour.

The power hour is the ultimate time to sell. You get a second wind, and your adrenaline kicks in as you try as hard as you can to close another sale. When you call with a group of callers in a room it's even better, because you can leverage the energy of the entire room and there is a sense of camaraderie. It can also be contagious—when one sales rep closes a sale it can give encouragement to the other reps. They believe they too can close a sale.

Some of the best prospects are the ones who are waiting for your call and don't even realize it. For example, you might dial homeowners who are trying to gather quotes for the very service you are selling. They are delighted that you called, because it saves them the long and tedious process of collecting quotes on the service they need. Another great example is when you call prospects who, coincidentally, are not happy with the service they are being provided by their current company. These two situations are what we call bulls-eye calls.

These prospects usually know what they need from your service, and they know what the general price range is and what they are willing to pay. There is very little introduction needed. You can get right down to business and talk about what your service entails, when you can perform it, and what it will cost. These calls truly feel serendipitous, and they can offer a huge relief to you when you hear the prospect on the other end of the line say, "I'm glad you called. I was just thinking about how I need to hire someone." This type of sale occurs frequently and can give you just enough of the boost you need to make the next sale. I even have the data to prove that one out of 100 calls will be a call like this. It really proves the power of numbers when cold-calling. This is why I am such a firm believer that anyone who really wants to be successful in cold-calling can be, just by working hard enough.

THE CLOSE SCRIPT

I am not a big fan of scripts, because they prevent sales reps from sounding authentic. Telemarketing has such a stigma nowadays that you want to be as far removed from that category as you possibly can be. However, I do recommend using a script for the close and for the sales wrap-up. Reading the close script will help you and your new client by ensuring that you are both on the same page. It is a concise review of everything you and your new client have agreed to in terms of service, schedule, and price. This is typically the tensest part of the sale, because it's often when prospects get cold feet and back out of the conversation.

In our company we do not have signed contracts with our residential lawn care clients, because contracts do not usually hold up in court. Additionally, lawn care programs are not a very high-cost service to sell, so it's not worth legally pursuing a customer who does not pay or breaks the contract in some way. If you choose to have signed contracts when you are selling over the phone, I would recommend purchasing a docusign software product so that you can email it and get the client's signature instantly. In that case, the deal is officially closed at that very moment. If you end up waiting, or if the client promises to send it back the next day, that is basically a polite way of saying no. This is why we record the verbal authorization portion of the close script.

The verbal authorization does not just serve as a verbal contract that solidifies the client's agreement to purchase the service. It also helps with overall communication. Buying over the phone can be confusing and distracting for consumers. They might be busy doing something else on the phone, or there might be background noise that makes it harder for them to hear you. On several occasions, I thought that the client and I were on the same page and agreeing on the same type of service, when in fact we were not.

My lawn care company performs seven treatments per season spaced four to five weeks apart. On a number of occasions,

I recorded the close script with clients who thought they were agreeing to a one-time service rather than the seven treatments that actually constituted the full service. On another occasion, a client thought that the price was for the entire year rather than per service. The close script can also clarify any misinformation you may have in your database.

For example, I was once closing a sale when I discovered the client had moved, so I had the client's old address in my database. Our service technicians would have ended up treating the wrong home, which could have lead to a whole other bucket of problems. The close script also provides the opportunity for sales reps to gather additional data from clients that can be used later for marketing and general communication. This includes email addresses and mobile phone numbers, information that will always improve the level of communication once you are servicing the client. Needless to say, confirming all of the necessary client information like this can avoid a lot of miscommunication and aggravation.

Whichever way you decide to work your terms of service, it can be a devastating loss for the sales rep if the prospect jumps off the line. To get to the close script on the sales call, reps typically have to invest 15 or 20 minutes of their valuable time, and it's not a pleasant feeling when the prospect jumps ship after that kind of investment. I liken it to fishing, when you get a big bite and the fish jumps off the line. So for obvious reasons you want to keep your same casual vocal tone and conversation flow when you transition to the script.

As a sales rep, you want to transition as lightly and carefully as you can, so that you don't spook your client. In our company, we refer to this as "bringing the customer to the register," and, just as in a retail store, the more quickly you get customers to the register, the more likely they are to buy your product or service. When you are transitioning to this part of your conversation, you want to avoid words such as *contract, obligated, locked-in,* or *binding* when you refer to the need to record the close script. I recommend that once you get a yes from prospects—when they agree to sign up for the service immediately—you transition as quickly as you can to their verbal authorization. At this point in the call, you want to make sure prospects feel comfortable and that you have overcome all of their objections and have answered all of their questions. Ensuring that you have done this makes it more difficult for them to digress and delay the recording of the close script.

You might want to say something like, "So with that in mind, we just need to record a verbal confirmation," or "Now that we have agreed on everything, we just need to record the remaining portion of the call for quality assurance," or "Now that I have answered all of your questions, I am just going to record the remainder of the call so I don't miss any of your information." In order to clearly record the close script, you also want prospects to speak up so that the agreement is clearly recorded and you know you are getting a solid agreement on service.

- I will be recording the rest of the conversation, okay? (Wait for prospects to say okay.)

- **Your first name is** _____. Correct?

- **You are the** homeowner at_____. Correct?

- **You are authorizing treatments from Noon Turf Care.** Correct?

- **The cost per application is $_____.** Correct?

- We have seven treatments a year and they are spread out three to five weeks apart, with free service calls if needed. We continue service from year to year unless we hear from you, okay?

- Would you like to set up our autopay program or prepay program and save 5 percent? I can take your credit card now.

- Can I have your email so we can send your program description and confirmation?

- We look forward to getting you started ASAP, and if you should have any questions or concerns, please call us at 866-547-LAWN (5296).

- Before I let you go, I wanted to let you know that we build our business on referrals. I can actually give you $30 off our service charge for each household that you refer to us and that signs up. Do you have any friends or family you think would benefit from our service?

- If they ask whether they can cancel at any time, tell them, "All we ask before you discontinue the service is to please call us and let us try to resolve the problem. That's fair enough, right?

CROSS-SELLING AT THE TIME OF SALE

Not only does a close script confirm the sale and clarify any discrepancies about what both parties have agreed upon, but it is also an ideal time to market other services your company offers. This is one of the few times when you have your new clients' full and undivided attention, so communicating with them about other services your company offers makes a lasting impression. For example, not only does our lawn care company offer lawn fertilization and maintenance, but it also offers a full line of pest control and shrub care services. In all of our close scripts, we ask new clients if they would be interested in receiving a free quote for pest control or shrub care, depending on the season and what services are in demand.

Asking clients at the time of the sale if they are interested in purchasing any of these additional services may seem brazen, but you would be surprised how much more a sales rep can sell when he simply asks. We usually make an introductory offer if a client chooses to bundle an additional service with our company. You might want to write something like this into your close script: "Well, now that we have your _____ service established, we also want you to know that we offer _____ service for $_____. Would you be interested in trying out this service as well?"

I have the statistics tracked through my call center that one in five new clients will purchase an additional service from us above and beyond the service they just purchased if the sales rep simply asks them. Even if they decline the offer, it creates a lasting impression on the clients, and I can't tell you how many times they will email or call us back when they actually need that up-sell service. They order it from us because they know it exists. Because they already know that we offer the service and we have already quoted them a price, it's just a matter of their picking up the phone or emailing us to schedule it. I am always astonished at how many business owners and salespeople I consult with think that the entire world knows what their company offers. I call it sales narcissism, and it is prevalent in many companies that I work with in this country.

For some reason, lots of companies build a culture of arrogance around their customers. They think that clients should be aware of all of the services they offer. The companies get upset when their clients use a competitor for a service they happen to offer. They think the client should be loyal to them and should purchase that particular service from their company. When I ask these salespeople if their existing customers are aware of the additional services they offer, they usually reply yes or "They should be." When I ask them why they think this is, they tell me that it's because these services are listed on all of their company literature, websites, and even emails that they use to keep in contact with their customers. I teach them that all of that still isn't enough.

You need to constantly remind clients and even ask them for more business than you are currently selling to them. I remember working with a lawn care company in Atlanta where the owner was having a difficult time selling additional services to his clients. For the majority of lawn care companies, add-on services provide the most profitable sales, because the companies are selling to their existing clients. Add-on services are even more profitable when you can up-sell them at the time of the sale. That is my idea of a true one-step sale or, as I call it, the one-and-done. When I was diagnosing one business owner's lack of add-on sales, I asked him a simple question, "Do your sales reps ask their clients for additional business?" After he gave me several vague answers, it was clear they did not. His reps were great at "marketing" these up-sell services to their clients, but they were not great—or even good—at "selling" to their clients. Within six months, we helped them turn this problem around. We instituted a process for his sales and service reps to always educate the client in order to fill their needs with supplemental services.

I tell my consulting clients to ask their customers for business until they turn blue in the face. The fact is, most times your clients don't know that you offer other services, and when you make them aware of this, they often forget soon after. When later the need arises for them to buy that service from you, it is out of their head completely. I will return to this point again later in the book when I review up-selling strategies.

ASKING FOR REFERRALS

Referrals are the ultimate sales lead, and they give you the introduction and endorsement you need to close your next prospect. I always tell my sales reps that it is very difficult to not close a referral. All you have to do is act professionally and live up to the expectations the person referring you has created for you. When I first started selling, I thought that referrals just came to you, like something that would randomly fall into your lap as a reward for hard work and professionalism. This can be true, but those are the easy referrals, the ones you have no control over. The referrals you have more control over are the ones you ask for. Yes, you read that right. You can ask for referrals, and no, you won't come across as desperate or tacky. It's all about how you ask.

My accountant taught me how to ask for referrals a long time ago, when we hired his firm to do our taxes and some consulting work. He gave us his sales presentation, and we hired him. Then, at the end of the meeting, he turned to us and said, "Well, I thank you for your business, and if you know any other young and successful business owners such as yourselves, I would appreciate you introducing our firm to them. We have built our company by bringing in new clients that value our work." Normally, I would have been a little put off by someone I had just hired who asked me to find more business for his firm, but I wasn't. This is because of the way he framed the question.

We all love hearing compliments about ourselves, and when he made one about us, he made us feel we were part of an elite group of business owners who "get it." In turn, I naturally wanted to contribute to this cause. Did I immediately provide him with referrals? Of course not! But he had planted a seed by asking me at our initial sales consultation when he had my undivided attention. Of course, once we had built trust and he had proved himself with real results, I was motivated to reciprocate by referring him to other business owners I knew. Asking for referrals is all about when you ask and how you ask. Once I implemented this approach in my own close scripts, the results were incredible. Every month our percentage of referral leads grew by double digits, and the volume of referrals compounded.

PHONE CHARACTER: THE DOG AND PONY SHOW

It is important to know that when you are cold-calling, you can be anyone you choose to be on the phone. I can't tell you how many sales I have made through the years by simply turning on the charm and entertaining my prospects so much that they decide to hire me just because they like me. I believe some of them would have bought anything I was selling. This is what I most enjoy about sales. Not only are sales prospects buying the product or service you are selling, they are also buying a little piece of you. The more they like you and feel comfortable with you, the more trust you will establish. And, as we all know, trust sells.

I once had a sales prospect who liked me very much and badly wanted to buy from me, but there was one slight problem— she didn't have a lawn. She agonized over this and finally came up with a solution. She would buy a lawn care program for her daughter's home. That is how much this woman wanted to give me her business. That is how much she enjoyed talking to me on the phone. In the same way a radio disc jockey's audience can't see the disc jockey, your prospects can't see you. They can only hear you, but they still form a bond with you if you deliver your personality, if you entertain them.

Like a great actor, you have the ability to bring to life any type of character that you think will increase your likelihood of keeping your prospect on the phone—you can formulate your own type of character and sales pitch to capture your audience's attention. Once you put that telephone receiver up to your ear and you dial that set of numbers, you are, as I say to my sales team, "live on the air." Once you are live, the dog and pony show begins and you are off and running. You need to consciously get into your positive phone messenger character. Remember that you are calling complete strangers and trying to persuade them to buy what you are selling. However, I want to make one thing clear. Creating a character on the phone does not mean lying or deceiving your prospects. Your message should be authentic and sincere, but you can be entertaining and memorable by presenting your prospects with a lively and colorful character.

For example, when I was starting out, I would tell my sales team that they have approximately 30 seconds to capture a prospect's attention and about 45 seconds to make their initial pitch. "You better be interesting," I would tell them. For us, our peak season for selling new lawn care programs is January, when there are 12 inches of snow on the ground and it is 20 degrees outside. Just imagine the level of enthusiasm one would need to sell a prospect on an evening like that. One thing that has made me and my company so successful at phone sales is the fact that we have never sounded like "traditional" telemarketers. You want to come across as representing a local company looking to earn business. Next, you want to come across as unthreatening as possible. By establishing a friendly character, you are humanizing yourself, and this encourages your prospects to let their guard down.

THE TELEPHONE INTRODUCTION

One of my favorite movie scenes about cold-calling comes from *Boiler Room*. Although I don't agree with the selling ethics of the characters in the film, I cannot deny that the characters were phenomenal at sales and the art of cold-calling. In one scene, Seth Davis, the main character, is at home eating breakfast and reading sales literature for the stockbrokerage where he had just been hired. The phone rings. It is a telemarketing company calling to sell him a newspaper subscription.

> Telemarketer: Hi, Mr. Davis, this is Ron calling from the *Daily News*. How are you doing this morning? *(Ron sounds as if he is reading from a script, and he mispronounces Davis's last name.)*

> Seth Davis: It's Davis, and I'm not interested.

> Telemarketer: Okay, I am sorry to have bothered you. Have a nice day.

> Seth Davis: Wait a minute. Wait. That's your pitch? You consider that a sales call?

> Telemarketer: Well, um …

Seth Davis: Ya know, I get a call from you guys every Saturday, and it's always the same half-assed attempt. If you guys want to close me, then you should sell me.

Telemarketer: All right ...

Seth Davis: All right. Start again!

Telemarketer: Okay. Hi, this is Ron calling from the *Daily News*. How are you doing this morning? *(The telemarketer repeats his introduction with more enthusiasm and a less robotic tone.)*

Seth Davis: Shitty! What do you want? *(He says this as he playfully laughs.)*

Telemarketer: It's not what I want. It's not what I want, sir. It's what you want.

Seth Davis: Ron, now we're talking. What are you selling me?

Telemarketer: I am offering you a subscription to the *Daily News* at a substantially reduced price. We are trying to reach out to people that have never had home delivery before.

Seth: So basically, you are saying that everyone who already has a subscription is getting screwed on this one?

Telemarketer: Yeah ... I guess so. *(The telemarketer replies reluctantly.)*

Seth: All right. Well, I can handle that. So tell me. Why should I buy your paper? I mean ... you know ... why ... Why shouldn't I get the *Times* or the *Voice* ... You know?

Telemarketer: Well, the *Village Voice* is free, sir. So, if you want it, you should certainly pick it up. But the *Daily News* offers you something no other paper can: a real taste of New York. We have the best features, more photographs than any other daily in New York, and we have the most reliable delivery in the city. Now what do you think?

Seth: You know what I think, Ron? I think that was a sales call. Good job, buddy.

Telemarketer: So you gonna buy a subscription?

Seth: No, I already get the *Times*.

What I like most about this scene is that it truly simplifies how easy cold-calling is once Ron tweaks his introduction and pitch. Like a musician who plays his music well, phone reps need great rhythm and timing. Although Ron did not get the sale, he received some very valuable training for free from a natural-born salesman. I can guarantee that if he applied what he learned from that phone call, he would go on to quadruple his success in selling that day. I use this scene to teach and train my new sales hires. It's effective training because it covers every step of the phone sales process, which can be broken down line by line and taught to novice sales reps. It's also nice to use a popular film with some comedic relief to get your point across.

Below, I will cover the entire process of the cold-call and pitch. Once a salesperson masters this process, it will begin to flow naturally like a song or story. This cold-call sales process is what every salesperson must master on every phone sales call.

1. The introduction (the icebreaker)

2. The probe (probing questions asked by the rep)

3. The pitch (presenting and laying out all of the benefits of buying from the rep)

4. The close (asking for the sale)

Phone Scripts

When I consult with sales professionals and managers, they most often ask for phone sales scripts. Although I believe scripts are great for training purposes, I don't require my sales team to use scripts when they are actually selling on the phone. I recently read an online National Public Radio article about Olympic bobsledding written by Robert Smith titled *In Bobsled, 'You Learn As You Go.'* It is amazing how similar the learning curves are for bobsledding and cold-calling. Just like an Olympic bobsledder, you truly need to learn as you go. There are no rules about what you can or cannot say, as long as you are honest and professional. I believe scripts make you sound like a robot and unsure of what you are selling. The last thing we want to do is sound like many of the national telemarketing companies. I think that if you know your company's products and services well enough, you will speak much more naturally and sound at ease without a script. Your prospects will notice how self-assured you sound, and that will instill confidence and trust in them.

I have listened to live calls and to recordings of thousands of calls made by my telesales reps, and the ones who sound the most self-assured and confident always end up being the most successful. The heavyweight boxer Mike Tyson once said, "Everybody has a plan until they get punched in the face." I love this quote because it perfectly describes the feeling of cold-calling. Everyone has a script ready until caught off guard by an objection from the prospect.

Ice Breaking

A couple of years ago I had a new sales rep who simply could not properly break the ice on the phone. Upon quickly diagnosing his issues, I found that he had the most trouble with a seemingly easy part of phone sales: the introduction. He would either get hung a few seconds into the call, or he would launch into his pitch the second the prospect answered the phone rather than first establishing a rapport. This is exactly what you should not do. I think it was just nerves that got him into this state of robotic speaking. Just as with any phone conversation you have, you need to break the ice first. As I jokingly tell my new sales reps when I train them, you need to have some "phone foreplay" before you launch into why your prospect should buy your service or product.

Remember, you are simply calling the neighbor of one of your clients and delivering a message. You need to take the sales call one step at a time. The steps are as follows:

1. Introduce yourself.

2. State the reason for your call.

3. Ask your initial probing question.

You have only an instant to establish yourself as someone worthy of not being hung up on when you cold-call. For example, when I first started cold-calling, I would tell my prospects that I was a local lawn technician and that when I was servicing their neighbor's lawn, I noticed that they had weeds in their lawn. This, of course, was true because every lawn has weeds in it. But with one sentence, I also accomplished three very important things, all within 30 seconds of breaking the ice on the phone:

1. It established my credibility as a lawn technician.

2. It established trust in me as a representative of a local company.

3. It created an icebreaking topic about the prospect's lawn.

It also drew an image of me in prospects' heads as representing a local lawn care service. That instills a sense of familiarity, which disarms prospects and keeps reps from sounding as if they are employed by some large telemarketing company, which, in fact, my company is not. I refer to this type of sales as "guerilla telesales," because it gives a personal feel to something that can often be very alienating for a prospect. The following is a typical 30-second pitch based on what I have just discussed.

The 30-Second Pitch

Ring, ring …

Prospect: Hello?

Salesperson: Oh hello, Mrs. _____. This is Chris calling from Noon Turf Care, How are you today?

Prospect: I'm fine, Chris. How can I help you?

Salesperson: The reason for my call is to let you know that I was in your neighborhood last week fertilizing my customer's lawn next door, and I noticed that you had some weeds in your lawn. What is your plan for the lawn this year?

Another example, for a cleaning service:

Salesperson: Oh hello, Mrs. _____. This is Chris calling from Noon Cleaning Service. How are you today?

Prospect: I'm fine, Chris. How can I help you?

Salesperson: The reason for my call is to let you know that we clean several houses on your street and, because of this, we can offer a discounted rate for neighbors. How are you currently handling the cleaning of your house?

These simple introductions almost always establish the groundwork for a pleasant phone conversation with your prospect. I often chuckle when people unfamiliar with phone sales ask me how I handle being hung up on so often in the job I do. The fact of the matter is I rarely get hung up on, because when I call prospects and break the ice, I sound like a friend or neighbor versus a telemarketer. Breaking the ice is all about the introduction. If you sound like a robot reading from a script, your prospect will hang up on you, guaranteed. You do not want to sound like a telemarketer calling from a gigantic call center. It's all about the first impression. If you deliver your icebreaker in a friendly and casual manner, your prospects will never hang up on you, because you have created a feeling of familiarity for the prospect, and you have humanized yourself by establishing credibility.

Many times when prospects who have been conditioned to take sales calls want to get you off the phone immediately, they reply in a very firm manner, directly after your introduction, with words such as "Not interested," or "We're all set." You want to get three no's from them early on in the introduction to be sure that they really aren't interested and aren't just putting their guard up. If you don't get a third no, keep pushing forward. Most times these immediate responses will not allow you to communicate what you are offering. This is very common, and it should not deter you or discourage you.

These responses are a polite way of telling you that the prospects aren't in the mood to buy. To confirm this, you should make a second attempt to politely steamroll them. *Steamrolling* is a popular term in politics, and basically it means that you politely brush off the prospect's response and proceed to quickly probe them to see if you can grab their attention. A rebuttal you can use to counter their claim of not being interested could be, "Okay— just to let you know—we are offering some great preseason rates on lawn care," or "Okay—just to let you know—our crew will be in the area seal-coating your neighbor's driveway, and because of that we are offering some one-time discounted rates." You want to mention any quick details that you can about what you are offering in order to engage prospects in a dialogue.

If they again say, "Not interested," you may want to proceed to a yes-or-no question to bring the conversation to a head. Examples of those questions are: "Do you currently have a lawn care service?" and "So you aren't interested in saving money on your lawn care this year?" Many times these last-ditch efforts will do one of two things: they will keep the conversation alive and relax the prospect so you can start your sales pitch, or they will further annoy the client. From there, you will know what direction to take the remainder of the call.

Qualifying the Buyer

You can't sell something to someone who doesn't have the authority to buy it. This sounds logical, but that information can be very difficult to get when you are selling on the phone. I can't tell you how many times, when I was starting out in sales, that I spent 10 or 20 minutes pitching someone who answered the phone and wasn't qualified to buy. There is nothing worse than thinking you are about to close a sale with a prospect who sounds interested and then discovering they are the babysitter, the wife, or even the daughter or son of the homeowner and don't have the authority to buy your service.

When this occurs, it can be really deflating, turning a good evening on the phone into a bad one. You always want to screen your prospects on the phone immediately after you break the ice and before going into your sales presentation. You want to be careful about how you present your screening question so that you don't scare a prospect off, so ask it casually while you ease into your sales pitch. By sounding too official or serious, you raise a red flag that indicates you are about to "sell" something to them, causing them to raise their guard and lose interest.

So you want to present the question casually, using language along the lines of "So are you in charge?" or "Do you have the authority to make purchases?" or "Do you make the decisions, take care of the _____?" I have always tried to keep it light when selling lawn care. I will ask, "So are you the lawn boss?" or "Are you the head groundskeeper?" This is a playful way to find out whether a prospect has the authority to make buying decisions. If they say no, you might ask why not. If they say yes, you can make your presentation, and once you have piqued their interest, you can qualify them. The reason for all this is that you only have so much time, and when you are on the phone dialing all day and night, your time is precious. You do not want to waste it on people who have no power to make decisions.

I believe that not qualifying your buyer is a form of laziness in sales and that when you fail to qualify your prospect you are only cheating yourself. Qualifying the buyer can sometimes be more challenging than one realizes, because some households don't even know who the buyer is. In fact, many times it really is a gray area for couples, and you can get caught in the middle. The question of who is in charge of purchasing home services can turn into a battle of the sexes, and that is a battle you don't want to get in the middle of. I am sure I have broken up a few marriages in the past by selling to the wrong person. The bottom line is that not qualifying prospects costs you and your company money.

I remember one time I sold this really nice and pleasant woman a lawn care program. She was very informative, asked a lot of great buying questions about our lawn care service, and finally purchased the program from me. I just assumed that she had the authority to do so, and I never bothered to qualify her. The next day her husband called our office, screaming. He told me to cancel the service and never to call their home again, explaining that he was in charge of the lawn care at his home and that he actually did the lawn care work himself. I think he was offended that his wife had outsourced his job. Whatever the case may have been, I upset a prospect who was now never going to buy from us, and it cost me a sale and 20 minutes on the phone the prior evening. The lesson to this story is to qualify your buyers.

If the homeowners make this type of decision together, try to see if the other spouse can also get on the line or arrange to call back another evening or on a Saturday when they are both home. Not only should you qualify prospects to see if they are authorized to buy, but you also have to qualify their home to see if your service is actually something that can benefit them. I can't tell you how many times I have witnessed one of my sales reps trying to close a customer before performing due diligence. One case in point is when a rep discusses a product or service and the prospect says yes to everything. The sales call is going really well, until the rep moves on to close the sale of the lawn care program and discovers the prospect does not have a lawn. Oops. Yes, this actually happens more often than you would think.

Another similar situation occurs when the rep has laid out the program for the lawn and thinks the call is going well until the prospect interrupts him to say, "Oh, I live in a condominium complex. I can run it by our board, but I am not in a position to buy it right now." This is a complete waste of a sales rep's time and very frustrating. Even if it only takes ten minutes of the rep's time, that is a lot when a rep sells for only eight hours per day. When one of my sales reps doesn't properly research his prospects, he has already built up hope in selling them, which can further deflate him when he learns that a sale is not possible.

Another way to qualify buyers is to see what their commitments are to any another service providers. Are they currently subscribing to similar services from another provider? You want to ask them if they have signed a contract and for how long. Some providers of home services offer a prepayment option at the beginning of the year, which makes it difficult for you to sell your service.

The laws for service contracts and prepayment refunds vary from state to state, so I recommend that you check the laws in the state(s) where you are selling. In some states, contracts for lawn care and other home services cannot be enforced, so consumers can get out of them fairly easily and make the switch to your company, but even if they don't have a contract you need to clarify that prospects are willing to switch to your company from their existing one. So you want to always ask a few times before you lay out your entire sales presentation. You want to make sure that your prospects are qualified to buy and that their home can actually benefit from the service.

Leveraging the Neighbors

A few years ago my family and I moved into our new home. It's located in a typical American suburb outside Boston, where the homes are well maintained and the landscapes perfectly manicured. As new homeowners, my wife and I had a hundred things to do when we moved in. Aside from all of the renovations we were doing, we had to also get the basic service companies hired to mow the lawn, clean the septic tank, pick up our trash, and so on. I was pressed for time when I needed to contact all of these service companies and gather quotes. So what did I do? I turned to the neighbors for a little help. My logic is, I live in an upscale neighborhood with well-educated people who are most likely similar to most New Englanders, meaning they are frugal. My neighbors were all very helpful in providing me with references, and I ended up hiring most of the companies they recommended, the same ones they used themselves.

One company in particular reinforced my philosophy of how powerful neighborhood references can be. It was the neighborhood garbage collection company. As I drove down the street one day, I couldn't help but notice that the streets were neatly lined with the same yellow trash barrels at the end of every driveway. Every single one of my hundred or so neighbors had hired the same trash service. It was surprising that in such a commoditized industry this trash company had leveraged the power of neighbors by giving the entire development a special rate to lock them all in. There are probably dozens of trash companies that service the area, but it was just easier for residents in the neighborhood (now including me) to hire the company that everyone else had hired.

Neighbors and references have always been a favorite topic of mine for breaking the ice and establishing credibility. As humans, we have a natural desire to belong and to be associated with others through, for example, social circles, neighborhoods, or associations. We want to belong, and we want to connect with people. Finding a common connection with someone builds immediate trust. Businesses love referrals, because the person who gave the referral has already "sold" the prospect by the time the prospect calls.

In cold-calling, our company is always making references to the prospect's neighbors. This establishes that our company is local and that the prospect's neighbor has already validated our service by hiring us. At my company, our phone software actually prompts our salespeople with a list of neighbors closest to the prospects they are calling. I will revisit how to create a neighborhood sales campaign later in this book. Making your introduction on the phone using a neighbor reference could go something like this: "Hi Mrs. Smith, this is _____ from _____ (company name). My company currently fertilizes your neighbor's lawn at _____and _____, and I thought it would make sense to contact you as well. Since we are already in the neighborhood, we can offer you the neighborhood rate of _____."

There is no better way for you to create immediate credibility for yourself with a prospect. If you don't service the prospect's neighbors or the area you are making your calls in is new to you, I would recommend referencing clients in the same neighborhood or even town. I will go as far as referring to past clients who are neighbors of the prospect—anything to create some familiarity. Rarely does a prospect even check the reference. It just helps you get to the important part of your sales pitch.

Adding Urgency

I have always been fascinated with the success of the home shopping industry. Sometimes, when I am surfing television channels, I stumble upon one of these networks and wonder who would buy their offerings, such as a knife that can cut through a penny or a stain remover that can remove any stain from a table-cloth. The two largest home shopping networks in the industry, QVC and HSN, ring up a combined $10 billion of revenue per year.

My point is, someone is actually buying merchandise from a television program, and the concept is hugely successful. I think the reason for this, aside from convenience and novelty, is that this industry is brilliant at applying the correct strategies to capitalize on the impulses of consumers. Most of these companies apply the technique of urgency to whatever they are selling. They emphasize that there is a finite supply of their product and a time limit on the special sales price they are offering, so customers must buy the product immediately, before it is out of stock, or the special price offer expires. The flashing red numbers displayed on the television screen, advertising the temporarily reduced price of the product, trigger in consumers an urge to pick up the phone and buy.

Not only will the discount end in a matter of hours, when the program is over, but the limited supply of whatever is being sold will run out as well. By focusing on the consumer's fear of loss, these television programs motivate consumers to buy immediately. This is why direct response marketing is so effective and why there are dozens of television channels dedicated to selling the latest and greatest cleaning solvents or commemorative coins. Fear of loss is one of the strongest emotions, overcoming logic in most people. After all, many of the consumers buying products from these programs fear losing out on a deal they didn't even know existed five minutes before turning on their television.

Now that you have learned why adding urgency to your message—by limiting the supply and/or the duration of a discount offer—motivates consumers to buy, you should understand why it is critical to the success of any cold-calling campaign you implement. Unlike order-taking sales leads, proactive cold-calling has to include an element of urgency similar to the direct response marketing techniques seen on television. Again, my formula for success on the phone isn't a matter of selling leads; it's a matter of selling sales!

Seasonality

So how do you add urgency to what you are selling to someone who just picked up the phone? It obviously depends on what you are selling. If you are selling lawn care, you can use the change of seasons to add urgency. In our company in New England, we add urgency by focusing on the start or the end of our season. We might tell prospects, "With the approach of spring it is critical to have your pre-emergent crabgrass control applied by early April. It would be wise to schedule this today so you don't miss that window of time," or "We recommend aerating and overseeding New England lawns in mid-September for best results in grass germination, and we can arrange to have it done by then if you want to sign up with us today."

If you are an irrigation contractor, you may want to say, "We strongly recommend blowing out your sprinkler system by the end of October to prevent your system from freezing. We have a few more spots open for early October if you agree to schedule this today." If you are selling exterior painting services in the summer, you may want to say, "Having your home painted at the peak of the dry summer is the best time, and we have a few more slots open for the last week of July if you agree to schedule today. If not, you risk rain spoiling your painting project if you leave it until the fall." Leaning on the change of seasons works for most services in most regions of the country. Weather is a challenge that most consumers can relate to. After all, in most cases, nature is beyond our control.

SCHEDULE

Another way you can add urgency to your sales pitch is by referring to when you can perform the service for your prospects. The almighty work schedule is a favorite go-to of mine when I need to put some light pressure on the prospect. Most sales reps who are selling for companies that provide residual services, or repetitive services, will have an easy time leaning on this method. It is a way to apply a little pressure without coming across as a typical high-pressure salesperson. For example, when we are selling new lawn care services to prospects over the winter, we refer to "supply and demand." We say something like this: "We have one of our best lawn care technicians assigned to your area, and right now he is almost at capacity for this season. We have a few remaining slots open, and if you sign up tonight, you are guaranteed to have a spot on his schedule this season."

If you are selling lawn mowing, you might want to say, "Your home happens to be located on our Friday mowing route, which is the day most often requested by our clients to have their lawn mowed. If you sign up tonight, I can guarantee you that day so your lawn is nicely mowed for the weekends this summer." If you are selling a one-time service, such as roofing or driveway seal-coating, you could say, "Our crew is working in your neighborhood until next week, so we can provide you this low price until then, but once our crews and their equipment move on to their next jobs in another area, that price will no longer be available." Referring to the schedule of whatever you are selling paints a realistic picture for the consumer and emphasizes your lack of control in the matter. You are now creating urgency, not as a pushy or high-pressure salesperson but as an advocate trying to get your prospect the best deal and the quickest turnaround in service.

FLEETING DISCOUNTS AND OFFERS

Offering discounts or free services to persuade a prospect to buy is another fantastic way of adding urgency to close a sale. In fact, I think it's absolutely necessary to offer discounted services when implementing my One-Step Sales strategy. You have to remember that when you make calls in a brand-new market, most prospects who are not referrals will not have a clue as to who you or your company is. Although you should always sell on benefits (which I will address below), you also need to have an offer that will grab a stranger's attention. Keep in mind that most qualified buyers (who are already using a similar service) will be happy about—or, at the very least, indifferent toward—the company they are using, and you are competing for their business. In general, people do not like change, even when they will benefit from it. You need to motivate them to make the change by offering them an incentive.

My lawn care company reps say, "I realize making a change is not always easy, but if you agree to try our service today, we will also provide you with a free lime application this fall as a thank-you for trying us out." If you are selling an alarm system service, you might want to say, "If you are willing to make the switch to our service today, we will give you the first month of monitoring for free so that we can build trust first." Most times, you can even find creative ways to recoup the loss of billing revenue and profit by promoting discounted services.

For example, my lawn care company offers free supplemental services to accompany our fertilization and weed control services. The free services can be combined and mixed with the existing fertilization services customers have purchased, and thus we can save money on product and labor. It is really a win-win when you can promote a product or service by giving it away for free but then save in other areas. We do this in our company by saving on labor and product when we offer the two-in-one free service.

Another way we can add urgency is by simply watering down the pricing. This might sound like a bait and switch, but it actually is not. Since we cold-call in the winter to schedule service for the spring, our company offers lower overall pricing for the purpose of scheduling. Every year, on April 1, we issue new in-season price charts or, as we call them, full-retail price charts, and we increase the pricing by more than 10 percent. When clients call to hire our company on April 1 and beyond, they receive those higher price quotes. After all, we have already filled most of our service vehicles to capacity, and it comes down to the simple law of supply and demand. In the winter, we can add urgency by explaining to our prospects the advantages of buying in the off-season.

My sales reps do this best by drawing a parallel to other retail industries, saying, "It's like buying a snow blower in the summer. It's always going to cost less than in winter, the peak season." Those clients who hire us early in the winter for service the next spring are rewarded with lower pricing; the early bird gets the worm, as they say. Watering down the price can work in almost anything you want to sell over the phone. Once you are ready to disclose pricing, after you have had your sales presentation about the benefits of your product or service, you say, "So with that in mind, the price is normally $_____ [for lawn treatments, alarm system, pest control program, irrigation service, lawn mowing, or whatever else], but if you want to schedule this tonight with us, it will be $_____ [a lower price by 10 to 15 percent]."

This might sound a little hokey and gimmicky, but I have sold thousands of new customers by cold-calling, and it never fails to create the sense of urgency needed to close a new sale in one step. No one ever wants to miss out on a deal. Many times, they know that they could probably call our company back in a month or two and get the same price, but they never want to take the risk. Many times, clients will buy on this pretense as a matter of convenience. They realize the hassle that looking for service providers and gathering quotes from companies can be. They typically are educated buyers, and they know when they are getting a good deal and value.

MATCHING VOCAL TONES

It is also important to remember to speak slowly and clearly. You need to speak quickly enough to keep your prospects' attention but slowly enough so they can understand you. This is particularly true when you are speaking on the phone to older people. Sometimes they may sound upset or annoyed when you speak to them, but it's just that they can't hear you and you need to speak up. A common mistake that inexperienced sales reps make is becoming nervous and starting to speak as quickly as possible. The prospect can sense this nervousness over the phone, and it is a big turnoff. After all, people want to buy from confident and calm people.

As a sales rep, you also need to remember to match vocal tones. According to psychologist Albert Mehrabian, tone of voice makes up 38 percent of first impressions, and people feel more comfortable when their vocal tones are matched in a conversation. Matching vocal tone is just how it sounds. When a prospect speaks loudly or gruffly, you do the same. When a prospect speaks quietly or softly, you do the same. When I first learned this, I didn't believe it, but the more I applied it, the more successful I was in breaking the ice and keeping the prospect on the phone. The type of prospect I have had the most success in disarming this way is one with a deep and authoritative voice. I used to prejudge these prospects as people who did not want to be bothered, and I assumed I would never get anywhere with them on the phone. But once I started matching their vocal tone by speaking back to them in an authoritative tone, and sometimes even shouting at them to match their tone, they would actually listen to me and become more engaged in my sales pitch.

HANGING UP

One of my biggest frustrations in managing sales reps is training them not to want to close a sale too much. It's almost as if they become blinded by the hope of closing a sale, and they lose all of their survival skills and logic with this false sense of hope. It reminds me of an old high school friend of mine. He was that kid in school who always dated the most attractive girls. And not just one—if my memory serves me correctly, he dated all of them. He wasn't even the best-looking guy or talented at anything in particular. He was just supremely confident, which made him cool.

Cool is a funny thing when you think about it. When I asked Derrick what his secret was he said it was simple: people want what they can't have. He told me the less you try or care if a girl likes you, the more they'll desire to be with you.

It also doesn't hurt when you are already dating a popular and pretty girl. People always want what someone else has, and they want it even more once they realize they can't have it. People who try to be cool aren't cool—because they try. Part of being cool is about not trying, and that is exactly what Derrick Snyder didn't do: he didn't try. This relates to sales as well. Yes, you need to be aggressive and put in 100 percent to selling every prospect, but you can't want it too much—if that makes sense. So once you present your pitch, lay out the benefits, and overcome any objections, you are ready to close. After you ask for the sale three times, you should move on. Once you complete the process and get three no's from the prospect, you have to be cool like Derrick Snyder. You can't want it too much after that or you will come across as being desperate, and no one is interested in buying from a desperate person. No girl is interested in dating a desperate guy, either. Desperation is a turnoff in any situation in life.

I am extremely protective of my time on the phone, and I tell my sales reps to be the same way. There is nothing worse than listening to one of them trying for 20 minutes to close a prospect who—and I can tell just by listening—doesn't want to be closed and won't be closed. You need to have a sixth sense for this in sales, or you will waste a lot of time that could have been devoted to selling the next prospect. "Take a hint," I tell my reps. "They don't want to buy!" I make a point when I sell to keep my desperation in check, especially on nights when I have zero sales on the board. My phone personality is like Derrick Snyder's: "Yeah, I'm interested in selling you, but I am not going to die if you don't buy from me." You need a take-it-or-leave-it attitude, combining confidence in yourself with confidence in what you are selling, and this can be challenging at times when you are cold-calling. That's okay. You are up to the challenge.

PROBING QUESTIONS

We talked about qualifying the buyer earlier, but there is a further step that involves qualifying the buyer's situation. I can't tell you how many times I have witnessed one of my sales reps trying to close a customer before he has even done his due diligence. This is a complete waste of a sales rep's valuable time and very frustrating for him. As I mentioned earlier, even if it is ten minutes of the sales rep's time, it is significant when he is selling for only eight hours per day. The rep builds up hope that he will sell the prospect when the conversation moves along. Little does he realize that, because he hasn't properly probed his prospect, the unqualified prospect on the other end of the line is just being polite and doesn't know how to let the rep down easily. Unqualified buyers are those who do not have the power, authority, or capability to buy. You can find out if they are qualified by asking a few key scripted questions that will reveal the answer.

Once you have broken the ice and are in an established dialogue, the next step is to probe the prospect with the necessary questions in order to gather the information you will need to sell. Probing questions are designed to engage prospects in opening up about the needs or concerns they have regarding the service offered. These questions are usually open ended, so you are forcing the prospects to give specific and honest answers. This is also a great part of the sales process that will show you whether you are keeping the prospect's interest or not.

For example, if you are selling an irrigation service, you may want to ask, "How are you currently maintaining your irrigation system?" or "What is your current water bill per year?" The answers you receive will then give you the information needed to proceed and fill that client's needs. If the prospect responds, "Currently, we just have a company turn the system on and off each season," then you can reply, "Well, with our all-inclusive maintenance program, we do midsummer checkups to ensure that the timers on your system are set properly so you aren't wasting water. Wouldn't it make sense to have a service that includes this, free of charge?"

If you are trying to sell a pest control service, you may want to ask, "Where are you seeing the ant infestation?" or "What have you done in the past to handle your pest issues?" The answers you receive will then give you the necessary information to fill that client's need. Typically, the more specific and relevant the answer is, the more interested a prospect is in buying your product or service. When asking probing questions, you want to avoid yes-or-no questions. You want to save this type of question for the end of the sales pitch to bring prospects to a trial close (discussed later in this chapter), or if you know they simply are not interested, you can use yes-or-no questions to bring the call itself to a close.

You want to obtain the following information (questions listed below) when probing prospects in order to begin selling them on the benefits of buying your product or service. You don't necessarily need to find all of these answers, but you need just enough information to be able to lay out your sales presentation and reveal the benefits of what you are selling. The following are some of the questions you might ask to find the information you are looking for. These questions might sound basic, but you want to get this kind of information out in the open so you aren't wasting your time.

1. Do you currently fertilize your lawn?

2. Do you hire a service or do it yourself?

3. What company do you use?

4. Why don't you fertilize your lawn? [Do they value a home service?]

Below are a few examples of probing questions that we use at our lawn care company:

- What is your main objective with your lawn this year?

- How do you plan on achieving this objective?

- What has been the biggest problem you've faced with your lawn?

- What problems have you experienced in the past with your lawn?

- What are you doing to deal with these problems?

- How are you currently treating your lawn?

- What do you like least about what you're currently doing?

- What do you like most about what you're doing?

- What changes would you make to improve your lawn?

- What effect would this have on your present lawn?

- What would motivate you to change?

- What has been your experience with lawn care services in the past?

- How much would you be willing to spend to fix the problems with your lawn?

- Have I overlooked anything?

- Do you have any questions for me?

- If there are no other questions, are you ready to schedule our service?

Once you have gathered all of the information needed by probing your prospects, be sure to write it down so you don't forget what they told you. You will need this information for the next step: laying out the benefits of how your company can fill those needs.

SELLING ON BENEFITS

One of the hardest things in managing sales reps is teaching them to believe in the value of what they are selling. I am adamant on this point, especially with our company, because we are a business leader in our industry. We are constantly improving our company for our employees, vendors, and customers. This is not only written in our mission statement but also on our company walls and all of the training literature we distribute. It is not just something we just write or talk about, either. We demonstrate it in our actions on a daily basis. We truly "walk the talk" in the way that our leadership team works, the way we treat our employees, and most importantly, the way we treat our customers. We reward the behavior of exceptional service and quality through recognition and bonus pay. However, even with all of this, it can still be challenging to make our sales reps truly believe in our value.

Most home service companies are in an industry with a low entrance barrier, thus making competition very tough. We constantly fight the commoditization of our services and business by being better. We don't cut corners with anything at our company, and we face tough decisions every day to do this. We make decisions based on a long-term outlook versus a short-term one. All this is why I am constantly preaching our company's value to my sales reps. We are not a company that simply undercuts pricing or blindly matches competitor pricing. Our company builds its business and sales by proactively cold-calling prospects, so adhering to an above-market-price chart can be challenging at times. I have a lot of respect for my sales reps, as cold-calling is not easy, and cold-calling for a premium company just makes it that much more difficult. But as I tell my employees, if we start to water down pricing and our price chart, we will erode the fabric and quality of our entire business model.

This brings me to my main point: adding value to what you are selling. Outlining the key benefits that speak to the concerns your prospects have about the service you are selling is critical to your success. It is, basically, your way of further supporting and validating your company's value proposal. Selling on benefits is one of the most important parts of the sales process. It means laying out a complete presentation of why the service you and your company sells is better than that of your competitors, based on key attributes that will meet the prospect's needs. The more you educate the prospect on why and how your company delivers a better service, the more likely it is that you can price your services above the market rate, or at the very least not make price a deal breaker for the prospect. If you have not truly dissected and identified what your competitive advantages are in the service you are selling, I urge you to do so.

If this has not been clearly communicated to you by the company you are selling for, it is your responsibility to ask the management team for this information. I urge you not to make assumptions about the benefits of what you are selling. There are often hidden benefits that your service may offer to the client, so it's important to explore and know all of them. When you are selling on the phone, time is limited. A prospect can become impatient. Often prospects are multitasking while on the phone, talking to you and doing something else at the same time. You need to be quick and concise with your presentation. You will not have time during your pitch to list all of the benefits of your product or service, so you will want to refer to your notes about the challenges or needs that prospects communicated to you earlier in response to your probing questions. Having identified the needs through probing questions, you can now match those needs up with the appropriate benefits.

Because prospects will not want to hear about all of the benefits, I recommend referring to three or four—the ones that best address the issues the prospects shared with you while you were questioning them. Lay out the benefits that your company offers. Talk about the benefits that are unique in the industry or that provide a competitive advantage over what other companies offer. Below is a list of benefits our company offers, benefits that are above and beyond our competitors' offerings.

- Free service calls

- No binding contracts

- All of our products are organic based

- We spot-treat weeds as needed

- Your account is assigned one designated lawn consultant for the entire season

- Complimentary soil testing

- Courtesy call before each visit

- Scheduling

- Online account viewing

- 24-hour access

- Call center support—you always reach a live person

- Real-time property information available instantly upon service

- State-licensed lawn consultants

Green Light Challenge: What benefits does your company offer that add value?

BUYING QUESTIONS

The questions and concerns that prospects have about products or services are what we call buying questions. When you get to this point, you have won your second victory in your battle to close the sale. The first victory is, of course, getting through your introduction and icebreaker without the prospect hanging up on you. The first buying question you hear significantly increases your chances of closing the sale.

Five years ago I was lucky enough to recruit and hire one of the best lawn care salespeople in our industry. He worked for a national competitor of ours for about six years before becoming disillusioned about his future prospects at that company, so he decided to join our team. Shawn went on to sell lawn care services worth more than $750,000 per year at our company, all sold over the telephone. When I initially interviewed Shawn, I was not very impressed. His resume and all of the sales records he had hit at his last company had led me to expect a more extroverted individual than the person I was interviewing.

I was surprised he wasn't similar in attitude and personality to most of the salespeople who worked for our company. He was more reserved and less talkative. What I soon realized was that the thing he was selling on the phone was his phenomenal ability to listen. Yes, he did a good enough job breaking the ice and communicating with his prospects, but his secret weapon was his ears. Even some of the best, most seasoned salespeople struggle with their ability to shut up and listen to a prospect. Although being extroverted and talkative is a great tool for icebreaking and sales presentation, it can hurt even the best salespeople when it isn't complemented with an ability to listen. Unlike most of my salespeople, Shawn conserved his energy to listen and then took that information and used it to close his prospects. When he heard those buying signals, he was like Muhammed Ali in the boxing ring. He danced around the ring gathering the buying questions, then went in with jabs and upper cuts, pouncing on those buying signals like a prizefighter.

Not only was Shawn a great listener who could quickly identify buying signals and questions, but he also had an innate ability to sense when prospects were ready to buy by observing the energy and tone of their voice. When he heard what he needed to hear, he wasted no time closing those prospects. His ability to keep the conversation progressing with prospects he knew were going to buy was a true talent. On the other hand, he also knew how to quickly exit a phone conversation when he did not hear buying questions as he laid out the benefits of our service. These talents enabled him to manage his time wisely, because he knew his time was valuable and not to be wasted on anything but selling new clients. So what are the buying questions? Below is a list of examples of clear signs that a prospect is interested in buying:

- How much is the service?

- How long does it take for the product to take effect?

- How long has your company been in business?

- Do you carry insurance for your business?

- Do I need to be home when you service my property?

- What is the frequency of service?

- When would you begin service?

- Do I have to sign a contract?

- What's included?

- Do you service any of my neighbors' homes?

The better you are at identifying buying questions, the more quickly you will be able to make a sale. This makes you more efficient with your time, and as I've said many times throughout this book, time is money. Buying questions are signals that prospects send to you. They send them because they are interested in what you have to offer. It is their way of saying, "Yes, I'm interested. Tell me more." The quicker you are at identifying these buying questions, the more successful you will be at selling the prospects.

CHAPTER FIVE

TRIAL-CLOSING

Remember this is *telesales*, not *telemarketing*. My system sells sales, not leads. As I preach to my sales team, every single phone number we dial is a lead. Trial-closing is one of the most important parts of my One-Step Sales system. The idea is to have the prospect make a series of small decisions rather than being confronted with one large buying decision at the end of the phone conversation. As you trial-close, you are also speaking in terms of "assuming the sale." You use language that indicates your intention is to sell your service on the telephone that very evening. It's important to make it clear to the prospect that this is the way your service does things, and when you are challenged with objections to your sales method, anything other than this system will seem surprisingly foreign to you—an attitude that will help keep the conversation moving toward the close.

In essence, you are gradually working up to the zenith of the sale, like a crescendo in music. Right from the beginning of the phone conversation, you say, "and I am calling this evening to schedule" rather than "I am calling this evening to sell." As the conversation progresses, you continue to speak the language of closing the deal that night rather than the next day, week, or month. You say, "*When* we schedule this service *tonight*" rather than "*Should* you choose to buy from us *at some point*." We are not selling or signing up or committing. We are scheduling.

You need to place deadlines on your service offer so that as you trial-close them, your prospect knows that what you are offering is only valid that evening and not the following month or week. Of course, you would honor the offer in the future, but trial-closing will decrease the chances of the prospect postponing the purchase. Just as with any effective negotiating, you want to propose the best-case scenario for yourself, as a sales rep, first, and you want to use language that will assume this outcome. Below are questions you will want to ask in order to trial-close:

1. Wouldn't it make sense to schedule this service at your home?

2. Do you have any other questions before I schedule this service?

3. So do you now understand why it is so important to use _____ at your home?

4. What would be the best day for you to have this service performed?

5. What credit card or debit card would you like to use to pay for this?

6. Would you like to sign up for autopay or prepay for this service?

7. What is your email address so I can send you the service agreement?

OVERCOMING OBJECTIONS

Sales objections are exactly what they sound like. They are reasons or arguments offered in disagreement, opposition, refusal, or disapproval of your sales presentation. Overcoming these objections is obviously necessary to making the sale. There are two or three objections you will hear when you are phone-pitching your products or services. As you become more experienced and confident on the phone, overcoming these objections will become second nature to you. In fact, you will begin to embrace these exchanges early in the conversation, because they are the only way you can get from your icebreaker to your closing. They are like a booth on a toll road. They are a necessary slowdown and a small price to pay for the use of an ultimately efficient roadway.

The better and more confident you are at overcoming objections, the more value you are adding and the more likely you will be to adhere to your pricing. Additionally, when you are successful in overcoming objections, you build trust with your prospects and are likely to sell more services in the form of up-sells. You always want to build trust by explaining the value of the product, and objections give you the opportunity to do just that.

Below, I review the most common sales objections a prospect uses to get off the phone and to ultimately say no to what you are selling. When facing any objections made on the phone, you will want to adhere to the following steps in order to overcome them:

1. Understand why prospects feel the way they do in not wanting to buy your service.

2. Acknowledge their concern.

3. Remove their concerns by explaining the advantages of your service.

DO-IT-YOURSELFERS

These are the homeowners who perform their own services for financial reasons, personal enjoyment, or simply ignorance of the fact that there is a cost-effective alternative to doing the work themselves. With the finite amount of time people have these days, it is becoming less common for homeowners to do their own home services. However, this has always been a very common sales objection, an easy fallback for prospects, so you need to be prepared. If prospects do the work themselves, it is important for you to find out why, so that you can narrow down how you will overcome this objection.

Many times when homeowners do their own home services, whether it's mowing the lawn, pruning trees, or washing windows, it's a matter of pride for them, even if they know deep down that they don't do a very good job. So it's important to approach these people delicately and with tact. The first thing you want to say is how you respect and appreciate the fact that they do it themselves. Second, you want to draw out the results they have had by doing it themselves and base your response on that answer. Below are four typical responses to use in overcoming do-it-yourself prospects' objections:

1. Cost:

This is one of the most common reasons do-it-yourselfers cite when asked why they do their own home service. Some people won't even admit that this is the reason, because they do not want to appear stingy. It is a common misconception with many home-owners that doing the work themselves is less expensive than hiring a service company to perform the same service at their home. As most small business owners and sales professionals realize, it is important to focus on the value of the services being offered, but the bottom-line cost to the homeowner cannot be overlooked, either.

In addressing objections about cost, it is important first to explore what the prospects are doing relative to what you are offering. You need to compare apples to apples so that you can break down the true cost for them. A few good questions to ask include: How often do you perform the service? What products or materials do you use? How much material do you use?

It is important to break down the cost of product as well as the cost of time invested in doing the task. Every year, my sales team actually takes field trips to large hardware stores to price out current costs of the fertilizer sold directly to end users. For those do-it-yourself prospects who have objections, we calculate the square footage of their lawn and determine the amount of material needed. We tally up the costs based on hardware store prices and give them the figure for comparison. In addition to the cost of materials and other products, there is the cost of time. Remember, homeowners have to get in their car and drive to the hardware store, purchase the material, products, and tools needed to do the task and then actually perform the service.

2. Quality of Products:

This is a great topic to bring to homeowners' attention. Many of the products that service companies use are professional or indus-trial grade. For services such as pest control and lawn fertilization, certain products are available only to licensed professionals and are unavailable in retail stores. Leaning on this fact is a fantastic way to add value and instill doubt in prospects' ability to do the work at the same level that a professional company can. They might start to think twice about the results they get from their do-it-yourself products.

Superior equipment is another advantage of a professional company. The equipment that technicians use will almost always be better and more efficient than what do-it-yourselfers use. Homeowners usually don't have access to the expensive equipment used by professional service companies. For example, our lawn care company uses golf-course grade lawn aerators, which do a much better job penetrating the lawn's soil (not to mention they can do the job 75 percent faster than a do-it-yourself aerator). It is important to remember when highlighting these points not to come across as an arrogant expert. You want to come across simply as a person who is trying to save the homeowner time and money while at the same time offering the services of professionals who will do a top-quality job.

Additionally, if your service requires calibration of a product, the technology of the commercial grade equipment used by professional companies will almost certainly be superior to the homeowner's calibration technology. Most products need to be applied with precise calibration to ensure that the technician (or the do-it-yourselfer) is not applying too much or too little of the product. Both can affect the desired results, so you will want to make this clear to the prospect by emphasizing the benefits of using this special equipment. You could also mention that it is better for the environment and minimizes the risk to the homeowner of exposure to harmful products because they won't need to mix and apply them. Remember, discuss only the benefits and advantages of your products and equipment, not the homeowner's limitations. You will get the message across without offending prospects if the message is delivered in that way. You will also be educating your prospects.

3. Guarantees:

Guarantees are another great way to persuade do-it-yourselfers to throw in the towel and try out your service. Homeowners who perform their own service cannot guarantee the results that professionals can unless, of course, they spend more time and money to do so. For example, if homeowners treat their home with retail pest control products or if they treat their lawn with retail grade products, and the desired results are not achieved, they will have to spend countless hours troubleshooting the problem. The only thing they can do is call the 800 number on the product bag or email the product manufacturer, and they still will have no guarantee of achieving the desired results, even if they have to reapply the product or do the entire job over again. As I tell prospects when I am selling for my company, "Our guarantee and our agreement are based on our results. If you are not happy with our results, we will work with you until you are." Framing the conversation this way takes the bite out of it for prospects and eliminates any risk in hiring our company.

4. Timeliness:

Let's face it, our clients are busy. That's why the service industry exists in the first place. Persuading prospects to be realistic about their own schedules is paramount to getting them on your side and buying your service. Many home services, such as cleaning, lawn mowing, gutter cleaning, pest control, and lawn fertilization are only effective if they are performed consistently and in a timely manner. For example, the pre-emergent crabgrass control we sell in the early spring is effective only if it is applied before the soil temperatures become too warm, because crabgrass seeds germinate in warm weather. So you will want to highlight how great your professional service is at timing the applications on a precise schedule for optimal results. You might want to say, "As you know, timing is everything in lawn mowing, pest control, weed control, and tree pruning. I am sure you are as busy as everyone else in the neighborhood. Signing up with us will guarantee that the service will be done in a timely and professional manner, which will give you one less thing to worry about in case your weekends become too full." And then you can remind prospects of a time they forgot to do the service you are selling: "Have you ever missed a week/month of _____? As you probably know, it's not pleasant when you have to play catch-up the following weekend, and meanwhile you have to look at the unfinished _____ all week long." Painting a picture with a familiar scenario will help you connect with the prospect, thus making the service you are selling far more desirable.

COMPETITORS

Calling prospects who are already using a service is another common hurdle, but it's a low hurdle. This is actually one of the best objections you can receive. The fact that the prospect already buys the service that you are selling instantly qualifies them for your sales pitch. Furthermore, these consumers are usually educated and familiar with your business, so you can move past the conversation of educating them on what you do and get right to talking turkey about what makes you better than the service they are currently using. This is why having a full understanding of the competitors in your market is one of the most important things you can do to become better at selling the specific benefits of your service. It is important because you need to sell on the needs that the prospect's current provider is not filling.

Of course, you can also ask prospects directly, but they will most likely be standoffish with you on the phone at first; they are not going to want to come right out and reveal the needs that are not being met by their current service. Only you can truly understand the benefits of what you are selling, and it will be much easier to connect with prospects if you already know what advantages your competitors are not offering. This could be in terms of pricing, service, quality, frequency of service, or other competitive advantages. You will want to politely say, "May I ask who you are using now?" to engage prospects in a discussion about what they like and dislike about their current service provider. They won't always divulge this information, but if you frame the question in a polite manner, many times they will reveal what you want them to reveal.

Selling these prospects on your value proposition and overcoming objections will vary, depending on which particular competitor they are using. For example, with our lawn care company, we provide soil testing for all of our clients who purchase a lawn care program, while many of our competitors do not offer this. With this in mind, you will want to say, "Well, I am sure your current service does a great job, but with our free soil testing we will be able to better understand the state of your lawn, which will then allow us to target our treatments specifically to your needs. This will, of course, come at no extra expense to you. It's a win-win."

Another example of our service advantages is that our company offers seven treatment visits while many of our competitors offer only five. Depending on the service your prospect is currently using, you might want to say, "While five treatments are good for your lawn, wouldn't it make sense to take advantage of seven visits to your lawn, so that you have a licensed technician on your lawn every month of the growing season, at no extra charge?"

The last advantage you can sell on is price. Although I don't recommend simply undercutting your pricing to sell prospects, it might be necessary if they are completely satisfied with the service they are currently using. You need to find a compelling and motivating factor to persuade them to undergo the hassle of switching services, and let's face it, everyone likes saving money. When you do sell on price, it is important to balance.

COMMON EXCUSES

You really can't blame prospects who rattle off a generic excuse for not wanting to buy or even take a phone solicitor's sales call. Let's admit it—we've all made an excuse at some point or another. The trick to breaking through these excuses will vary depending on the excuse used, but there are very common responses that you can use to break through to the next level of dialogue and sell prospects without their hanging up on you. It's important to keep in mind that these responses will require you to put some pressure on your prospects.

You will also need to be assertive in adding urgency to the call, as we covered earlier. The idea of high pressure does not sit well with many people. They have an ethical issue with applying pressure to complete strangers. I certainly understand their point of view, but I think in cold-calling it goes with the territory.

Through the years, some of my best customers were once prospects whom I had to yell at to get them to sign up before the deal I was offering expired or before our routes filled up. I admit that when I apply pressure to reluctant buyers, I have the attitude that "it's for their own good." The reality is that people procrastinate and often know full well that by doing so they are hurting themselves financially.

I can't tell you how many times a prospect has rejected my discounted service proposal and then called in several months later, looking for us to honor that price. I rarely honor the really low introductory offer at that point, and then they get to hear my "I told you so" speech. It may seem harsh, but it's the only way I can add value to what I'm selling. Of course, I make exceptions from time to time if there is wiggle room in the pricing. But our off-season pricing is the best, and to honor it after the expiration date that I once held over a prospect's head would make our company lose credibility.

It is important to know that many of these excuses really are a polite way for prospects to tell you no, but there is no way of verifying this except through the use of pressure. It is important to quickly identify the prospects who truly are not interested in what you are selling so that you can move on to your next call. Keep in mind that some people may just not be in the mood for buying. Like a window shopper who wanders around a store but does not buy, sometimes people are just not in the mood. Again, as I have stated numerous times before, it's a numbers game. You are simply trolling the phone lines looking for the prospects who do want to buy, so it's important to use your time and energy sparingly and on the right buyers. Below are some of the excuses you will hear. You will also see that the responses you can use to counter these objections are very similar, which makes it easier for you to remember them all.

I'm Waiting for Other Proposals

This is a common objection you will hear during the peak of demand for whatever it is you are selling. Sometimes it is an honest answer, and other times the prospects intend to gather other quotes but never end up doing so. Either way, you can make it a win-win for both parties—by eliminating the risk for the prospects if they agree to hire you that evening. First, compliment them for being an educated consumer and tell them that you appreciate what they are doing. Then encourage them to gather other quotes and to do so as soon as possible. To zero out any risk for them, you make an informal deal: tell them that you will schedule your service for them that night so that they don't miss out on the deal you are offering but that should they find a better price or another service they prefer to hire for whatever reason, all they need to do is call you back, and you will take them off your list.

I Can't Afford It

We started our lawn care company in October 2008, during what was arguably one of the worst financial crises our country has ever seen. There were days it felt like the sky was falling. At times like this you need to maintain a positive mental attitude and persevere. We really had to focus to make it through such a tough economic climate. I made it a point simply not to acknowledge the recession and to fight through it. I am a firm believer that when you are selling in tough times, the economy is only as bad as you make it. Selling on the phone, I clearly remember hearing one in five prospects tell me they were either out of work or having financial problems. When prospects weren't declining our sales offers on the phone, our existing customers were calling in to our office and canceling service because they had lost their jobs or had other financial setbacks with their investments.

Although some of those prospects literally could not afford the service at the time, many of them could, and it was our job to work through these objections by persuading them to see the value in the special rates we were offering that day on the phone. When you do reach prospects whose objection is financial in nature, you want to be sensitive to this. You want to be understanding and truly listen to the prospects' reasons. Once they have purged this personal information, it is best to thank them for sharing it. The next step is to eliminate the risk of their deciding to schedule service with your company. You do this by first explaining that the service agreement is not binding. It is simply a pay-as-you-go program that can be discontinued at any time.

For example, at our lawn care company, most of our sales, as I have mentioned, are made during the winter months. Our service does not actually begin until the following spring. So, in essence, a prospect would not be obligated to pay until then. So when someone says, "I can't afford your service right now," you want to reply, "Well, Mrs. Smith, the good news is you don't have to. All we are doing today on the phone is scheduling the service. You will not see a bill for this for months, until we perform the service this spring. In fact, all you are doing now is saving money by scheduling preseason, and since you will need to buy the service in the spring, doesn't it make sense for us to lock in your preseason rate today?"

Send/Email Me a Quote

Most sales reps think that when they hear "send me a quote" from prospects, it's a polite way of saying no. They are usually right about this, but it doesn't mean they can't convince prospects otherwise. If you think about it, these prospects have already committed to hearing your pitch, which means they have expressed the slightest inclination of interest. In other words, you have already done a lot of the heavy lifting and invested at least three minutes in discussing the service you are selling. So when I hear this line, I only hear the first no, and you need three no's from a prospect before moving on to the next call. "Send me a quote" only counts as one no.

The way you overcome this objection is by letting prospects know you just gave them a quote right over the telephone. The figure that was just discussed is the quote. You also want to let them know that your company does not even send out quotes, because you are a green company and the very reason you use the telephone is so you don't have to waste paper and postage. If prospects request a quote via email, you can tell them you will happily do so, but then you want to double back to add some urgency. You might want to say something like "I'd be happy to email you a quote, but—just to let you know—the price I am offering only holds for tonight. But what I can do is get this scheduled for you so your service route does not fill up. Should you decide against the service, simply call me back, and I will take you off the schedule. How does that sound?"

Unfortunately, the reality of selling over the phone really does require some pressure. Let's face it. Your likelihood of closing a sale in the future and not in the present while you have the prospects on the phone is slim. If this added pressure does not work, and your prospects still want a written quote, it never hurts to send an e-quote. I will come back to emailing quotes later in the book.

I Have to Talk to My Husband/Wife First

This is another common excuse used by prospects, and your response should be similar to your response to the excuse of "send me a quote." Most of the time, this excuse would have been flushed out when you qualified these prospects. You want to politely remind them that they told you earlier that they were the decision maker. Avoid being contentious, of course, so when you remind them of this, you might best play dumb, as if you were the one who had forgotten. Either way, you want to drive forward with the conversation and let your prospects know you respect their decision and you completely understand their position. Sometimes you can even say it with a little tongue-in-cheek remark to keep the mood light, saying, for example, "Oh yes, I completely understand. I am the same way at home. I don't even buy ketchup at the store without consulting my wife. A happy wife is a happy life, ha ha."

Moving on from there, you want to say, "What I can do to make it easier on everyone is schedule the service so that we can lock in that great discount, and then you can talk it over with your wife at dinner. If for any reason she does not want to move forward with the service, simply call me back, and I will be happy to take you off the list." This may seem unworkable. However, in my experience, nine out of ten times the prospects don't call you back. They keep the service scheduled. If they decline your offer, try to schedule a call with them later in the evening when the spouse comes home, or perhaps on a Saturday morning when they have time to discuss it as a family.

ASK FOR THE SALE

As many of you already know, the life of a salesperson can be very challenging at times. I think one of the worst aspects of selling is a sales funk, which is a period when you simply can't make a sale. It is during this time that you must keep a positive mental attitude and persevere until you make the next sale. If you don't make that sale, it can create a state of anxiety and panic for you. You can become superstitious; if you are not strong minded, you may start to blame outside forces. This period truly separates the men from the boys. It is important to stay focused when this happens and not lose hope, as you simply need to ride it out. It is also a time when diagnosing the cause of your dry spell becomes critical. I remember when this happened to a fairly new salesman at my company, named John G.

Around the fifth month after John joined our team, he hit a wall. It was a gloomy week in March, and he just couldn't sell a thing. He was going on his third day of goose-egging on the sales board when he approached me with his concerns. He began to make excuses for his inability to sell. He offered up all kinds of reasons for his consecutive nights of sales failure: It had been snowing all week; his callbacks weren't picking up the phone; all of his leads had made their decisions on their lawn care plans for the year. The list went on.

I decided to sit with him for the evening on the phone to help diagnose his problem before he slipped into a sales coma. Within about an hour I realized that, for some reason, he had stopped asking for the sale. His introduction was great, and his sales presentation sounded even better, but he could not close anything. It was as if with every rejection he received, the more defeated he became. After he had made a flawless presentation, rather than

140

ask for the sale, he would dance around the question and allow the prospect to delay his decision, and the call would turn into a callback. I knew all I had to do was break his fear of rejection and remind him of how good he was at selling. I did this by showing him.

When he was on his fourth or fifth qualified call with a prospect, I waited for him to make his pitch, which he did—and then I jumped on the phone line through phone management software and blurted out, "So will you give us a chance out there this year, fertilizing your lawn?" in a voice that I was trying to make sound as much like John as I could. Within seconds the prospect replied, "Sure. What the heck! Sign me up!" At first John was annoyed that I had cut him off, but his eyes lit up and his feelings turned to gratitude when I closed the sale. It never ceases to amaze me that even the best sales reps can fall into a funk. But I am convinced that even with a mediocre sales pitch, if you confidently ask for the sale you are much more likely to sell the client.

Asking for the sale is one of the last steps in the sales process. Once you have made your introduction, performed your sales presentation, and addressed any sales objections, you must ask for the sale. It should take about ten minutes to get to the close of the sale. I emphasize the time so much with selling because many newer sales reps think the longer they stay on the phone, the more likely it is the prospect will buy from them. This is simply not true. You don't want prospects to get too comfortable with you on the phone, because that can make them feel more comfortable with putting off making a decision or, even worse, saying no.

Once you lay out your sales presentation and answer any questions prospects may have, it is important to stay on task so that you don't drop the sale. I actually use an hourglass for training new reps. It runs for three minutes, so I guess you could call it a three-minute glass. Once that hourglass runs empty, the reps should be well into the pitch, answering any objections the prospects have. For my sales team, the cardinal rule of selling is to ask for the sale at least three times throughout the course of the sales call. Yes, three times! If sales reps don't get a yes or a no from the client, they have not done their job. They don't ask three times in row, of course, but they should ask for a sale after overcoming each objection. They must not be shy, and they must keep in mind that the worst thing prospects can do is say no.

I think that asking for the sale is more important than anything, not only in selling but also in life. Asking for the sale is essentially like asking for anything else. As I mentioned earlier, it is a skill that will make you good at negotiating, getting discounts, and even getting a date. I firmly believe that if you can become fluent and confident in asking, your potential in life has no ceiling. People naturally have a fear of rejection and failure. "What if they say no?" is often the little voice in their head that holds them back from asking for whatever it is they want. I believe that anyone can overcome this fear by simply practicing asking. The more you ask for the sale, the more likely you'll get a yes. The more you hear yes, the more your confidence builds.

It truly is a building process and, like a muscle, it strengthens over time. I have also found that as your "asking muscle" strengthens, so does your confidence. You will actually be able to hear it in your own voice. More importantly, the person you are asking will hear it, and as I have stated before, consumers love buying from confident salespeople. One of the best examples of this is in the movie *Crazy Stupid Love*. In this film, Jacob Palmer, the eligible and confident bachelor played by Ryan Gosling, is trying to teach the recently separated Cal Weaver, played by Steve Carell, how to ask women out and start dating again. Cal had been married for 20 years, so it had been a long time since he had gone on a date. In one scene, Jacob mentors him in the art of picking up women and asking them to go home with him. Like a seasoned salesman, Jacob makes it look easy and effortless to Cal. But the real secret to Jacob's success, other than his smooth pickup lines and natural confidence, is his ability to close the deal. No matter what the circumstance is, Jacob always asks the girl the same question at the end of the night, "You wanna get out of here?"

Jacob is successful in getting a yes from the girls he asks for two reasons. The first is how he asks. The way he frames the question is casual yet direct so as not to scare the woman away. It is as if the way he asks is "no big deal," which puts the woman at ease. The second reason is the way he asks her. He is supremely confident in assuming that she will say yes. Just as in selling anything on the phone, the combination of those two things will greatly increase your chances of closing the sale.

When asking for the sale, as it is with asking a girl to go home with you, the only thing that really changes is what you ask prospects. Either way, you are asking for a commitment. So how do you ask for the sale? You say something along the following lines:

"With that in mind, are you ready to take the next step in having a greener lawn?"

"Wouldn't it make sense to schedule this service today?"

"Is this something you want to sign up for?"

"Why don't we get this scheduled for you?"

"So how about giving us a chance out there this year?"

"So can we can we take the next step in giving you great results?"

In summary, asking for the sale is the last and arguably the most important step in closing the sale. It is important to ask for the sale with complete confidence and conviction to let prospects know that you believe what you are selling will, undoubtedly, be a good investment for them. If you have done your job in the previous steps of qualifying and overcoming objectives, asking for the sale should just be the next logical step. You should ask in a way that indicates you are assuming the sale will go through. You should ask in a tone that says any response besides yes would be ludicrous.

The prospects at this point in the conversation will have already made a series of small commitments to what you are selling, and the close should feel very natural. It is my opinion that if you have carefully followed these steps and have given 100 percent to your pitch, even if the prospects decline the sale you should feel satisfied that you did everything in your power to sell them. Either way, you will have received a definitive answer. You will have no doubts, which you would have had if you had neglected to ask for the sale. You will be left with the mental fortitude to move on to the next phone call, feeling confident and determined to close the next prospect who answers the phone.

CHAPTER SIX

BUILDING YOUR TELESALES STRATEGY

DATA UNIVERSE

The first thing you need to do when setting up your telesales campaign is create a data universe, which is your entire marketing database of every prospective customer in your market. Why do this, you ask? Because just like any other form of marketing and advertising, repetition builds familiarity. You will be calling the phone numbers in this database for years and will also use several other means of marketing to these customers. You want to build brand recognition—so that by the time you have called prospects for the fourth, fifth, or eightieth time, they know you and are finally ready to buy. Although cold-calling can work the first time you call prospects, your chances increase significantly if you have been flooding them with phone calls, emails, direct mail, and any other forms of advertising.

Think of it as if your prospects are hearing a radio ad every time your company calls them. Yes, you may irritate them sometimes, but just as an annoying relative grows on you, you will grow on your prospects. The other benefit of creating a database is that you can track how many times you have contacted and marketed to the prospects prior to selling them. This data will become increasingly valuable in deciding where you want to invest your marketing dollars as your company and marketing budget grows.

You can purchase prospect lists from various marketing companies that specialize in selling this information. You will be able to filter your prospects in just about any way you prefer. For example, we purchase single family residential listings in our target market that have a specified profile of home value, wealth rating, lot size, and other demographic indicators. I suggest building your own target market profile. In other words, ask yourself whom you are selling to and whom you are, ideally, looking for as clients. Is yours a premium service that only sells to certain people with a certain income level and home value? Or does your business cater to a wider demographic, and are you trying to target a larger volume of customers?

Only you know the answers to these questions, and once you have those answers you can move forward in ordering the appropriate data from a marketing company. After you have your database set up, you will want to cleanse it every year of people who sign up for the DNC list and of homeowners who move in and out of homes. This will ensure that you are getting the most value out of your data investment. The cost to do this is not substantial, and is well worth the investment to ensure that you have the cleanest information to work with. Because my company is so data driven, we even take this strategy a step further.

CUSTOMIZING YOUR DATA

When customizing your data, you can also go a step further by creating the most precise and detailed data. The more information you have about your prospects, the more likely you will be to close the sale. The basic information you need for adequate data includes wealth ratings, income brackets, geographic locations, phone numbers, and addresses. Going a step further means purchasing public information, such as home size or lot size. This is particularly important if you are in a business that builds pricing around the size of the home or lawn. These are relevant numbers for many home services. Having this information enables you to be quicker and more efficient in providing instant pricing to your prospect, which minimizes the lag time that would otherwise be necessary to obtain this information online or visit the property to price it in person.

For example, if you are selling pest control services and you already have the square footage of the home, and that data is attached to the rest of the client's information in the database, the price of the service would be right in front of you on the screen. In that case, you could instantly quote a price to the prospect. At my lawn care company we are so obsessed with time management and efficiency that we actually created an average lawn-fertilization service price for every homeowner in our database. We did this by creating an algorithm that takes the size of the homeowner's lot and then subtracts the driveway, woods, and home, leaving us with the approximate size of the lawn. That information is then uploaded into our client database and directly into each account we have set up.

Thus when our callers make cold calls, they have the lawn size right in front of them on their screen, and they can use that to provide an instant quote to the prospect. Sometimes the lawn size is not 100 percent accurate, but my reasoning is that we have beaten all of our competitors by quoting the client first, thereby increasing the likelihood that we will sell the account. In summary, the more information and data you have on your prospects, the more likely it is that they will buy from you. In my experience our close rate and lead generation rate increases by more than 50 percent when we market with customized data.

Another benefit to customized data is that you can use it for initiatives other than your cold-calling campaigns, thus killing two birds with one stone and maximizing your return on investment in your marketing and sales budgets. For example, as I mentioned, my company invests in the purchase of lawn dimensions so that my sales reps can instantly provide pricing to prospects right over the telephone at the time of the call. We also use this customized lawn-size data in our direct mail and email marketing campaigns. The actual lawn size and price of our service are included with each post card and email we send to our prospects in our constant contact campaign.

This greatly improves our response rate, because studies have shown that when you include customized information about your prospects they tend to relate better to your advertising. This is something that is executed especially well in the car sales industry. When car sales companies market to their prospects, they include the customized information and car mileage of the cars they are leasing. This triggers their prospects to act on the information because the personal information they received resonates with them and they feel they are receiving an exclusive offer. When you properly manage your phone analytics and data, you can also generate your own data that is of value.

Phone Software

Aside from your database, the phone software will be the largest and most important investment you can make in your telesales campaign. Years ago, when I first started selling on the phone, I used an analog autodialer. This technology worked well but produced high phone bills. Today dialing technology is mostly software based—no longer analog—and only requires an IP address to operate. This is truly a benefit, because as your sales reps grow in number there will be no additional phone charges, and the only wiring you will require is for setting up the computer and loading the software. The best phone software available allows sales reps to dial their prospects at the proper pace, as the software employs sophisticated algorithms to speed up and slow down the call rate based on the number of available agents, the number of available lines, the campaign's average call time, and other factors.

Autodialers automate the outbound calling process, allowing your sales reps to simply upload or compile lists, click start, and let the power dialer automatically call contacts, one after another, until someone answers the phone. The phone software does all of the work, so your sales reps can spend their time closing sales rather than hunting for prospects. Good software will automatically display comprehensive information about the prospect as soon as the sales rep places the call. The autodialer and caller information screen make the sales process more efficient, streamlined, and effective. Once the rep speaks to a prospect, all of the prospect's information will appear on the computer screen, so the rep will know the prospect's name, address, and customized information.

For example, depending on the marketing data you purchase, your agents can have access to lot size, house size, and even lawn size. Past notes, made by reps on previous sales calls, can also be logged on the account and visible to the sales reps currently speaking to the prospect. If a prospect is interested in continuing talks with you but cannot make a decision that day, you can simply log all of the information that was discussed on that particular call, along with pricing and discount promotions offered, and set your phone software to call that particular prospect back on the date and at the time you booked for the next phone meeting.

This technology, called *predictive dialing*, greatly improves the efficiency of a sales rep's time, because as the rep is speaking with a prospect on the phone the software is dialing the next phone number. So when the sales rep ends one call, a new prospect answers the next call. This creates minimum downtime and eliminates wasted time for your reps, something that traditional manual dialing can never do. Campaign settings are also designed to comply with state and federal regulations. I like predictive dialing because it takes the psychological element of cold-calling out of the sales rep's head. No manual dialing and no dial tones are involved. The rep simply plugs his headset in, activates the software, and begins his pitch when a prospect answers the phone.

The other advantage of this software is that it also gathers and utilizes analytical data. Phone reps can automatically enter the result of a call into any category. For example, my company's categories include: sold, not interested, call back at a certain time/date, and DNC (customers requesting not to be called again). Depending on the outcome of each call, sales reps also have the ability to enter notes explaining the status of the lead. This data can be compiled later and used for marketing campaigns or calling campaigns, which I discuss in more detail below. During one week, for example, you could mail, do an email blast, and call only those clients you have provided a quote for in the past—

investing your team's energy only in prospects who are already familiar with your service and have been given pricing by one of your sales reps. This increases the probability of closing these folks, especially if you couple these efforts with the peak of demand. If you are selling pest control services, you might want to contact the prospects who have expressed interest in your service but declined the offer in the past, reminding them of your previous offer and also that the season is now at its peak. They will be a lot more receptive to your services during the peak demand season when they really need them, such as the month of July when they have ants marching in and out of their home.

Sales Scripts

I briefly referred to sales scripts earlier in this book. Sales scripts are great for training, but as I mentioned before, once you have attained mastery in cold-calling, you will not need them. Like anything else in life, the more you practice and refine your cold-calling skills, the more your confidence will build. As an actor memorizes scripts and draws on his inner confidence and skill, a seasoned salesperson can cold-call with ease and navigate through a sales call intuitively, thus making it all sound natural and professional.

Recording Device

Investing in a quality recording device is very important when building a phone sales process. As I mentioned earlier, it is not necessary to record the entire conversation, although you can if you wish. The important thing is to record the last step of the phone sales process, which is the close script. The close script is important when you are managing a team or simply selling on your own. First, if you do manage a sales team, it ensures that the sales your reps are closing can be properly audited. This allows you to filter out any bad sales. Second, it keeps both parties on the same page with what the rep is selling and what the prospect is agreeing to. It can be confusing when you purchase anything on the phone, so having a recording device is essential. It acts as a verbal contract.

Many times, clients will forget what they authorized, so it is important to have evidence to build trust. Recording devices are built into most quality IP phone systems. However, you can also purchase a very inexpensive one for your computer. These are available online or at any local electronic retailer. Once you record the sales script and receive complete authorization from the prospect, you can then include this sales recording in the account provided in the service software you use. There is usually an area named "Documents" where you can attach it. This is also helpful for the service department, because they can check the recording throughout the duration of the service should they have any questions or concerns.

Analytics

The analytics tracked by a quality phone software program help you and your sales team better understand your performance on the phones. The software will track the number of phone calls made, the number of prospects who connect, the number of and type of sales rejections, and the number of sales made. It can also track how long you and your sales reps have been on the phone with each prospect, thus allowing you to better coach and manage your reps' time, based on authentic data. You can analyze when you and your sales reps are making the most contacts with prospects.

For example, my reps make the most contacts with prospects during the early and prime-time evening hours, so I will schedule my sales reps to call warm leads and make their call-backs during the earlier times of the day. This maximizes their efficiency, so there is little room for error. Analytics really prove their value to anyone managing and training a large team of sales reps. The numbers don't lie, and managing off this information makes the process very objective and removes unnecessary and sometimes unproductive emotion from the process.

CALLING CAMPAIGNS

Calling campaigns are one of the biggest benefits of a quality dialing software program. They are targeted to reach certain prospects and markets in your database so that you can directly control when and whom you call. For example, you could upload targeted lists from your database, including past customers, neighbors of existing customers, or prospects who have inquired about your company's service but have never hired you for one reason or another. Targeting a select group of prospects allows your sales team to focus and be better prepared to pitch and sell. You can also set up customized scripts that your sales reps can use to concentrate their efforts when they are contacting a particular type of prospect.

Another advantage of calling campaigns is that you can build them around your company's existing marketing efforts. For example, at our lawn care company we contact the neighbors of our existing customers soon after we send our trucks out on the first round of service in the early spring. This makes the cold call a little warmer, as these prospects will have had some exposure to our marketing prior to the call, creating more brand recognition.

These prospects will have seen our company trucks and signage while we were treating their neighbor's lawn, and they will most likely have seen our signs on their neighbor's lawn after treatment. They will have received a direct mail postcard with information about our company and a list of their neighbors that we service.

Neighbors

Contacting neighbors of existing customers is one of the most effective sales strategies for acquiring new customers. Leveraging references from your existing customers creates new sales without a lot of the traditional objectives you typically receive from cold-calling complete strangers. If you couple a sales call campaign with a direct mail campaign and signs at your clients' homes, you will have more exposure and more success.

By using calling software technology, you can upload specific database lists such as the phone numbers of people living in the neighborhoods where you are already working, or you can get as specific as locating the phone numbers of the direct neighbors of your existing clients. You can program the names and addresses of your existing clients into the software so that they appear on your screen, and you can use their names as referrals during your calls with neighbors. When you refer to your existing clients during a cold call, your prospects view you as warm and nonthreatening, because you are talking about their neighbors who just happen to be your existing, satisfied customers. This builds familiarity, which in turn builds trust.

Canceled/Past Customers

Clients who have discontinued service for whatever reason also make excellent lists for calling campaigns. Many companies I consult with have thousands of clients, which means that statistically, they have hundreds of past customers floating around in their database. The ex-client needs to be reached out to, and you can easily do this by uploading all of your canceled client data into your predictive dialer. Again, having your entire sales team call one particular list at a time builds momentum and energy in the room, as each sales rep overhears another rep speaking to prospects. It builds camaraderie and inspires the troops as they work through these calling campaigns.

Cancels are low-hanging fruit in the world of sales. There is little introduction needed, and your sales reps can get right down to business in reselling these customers from the past who could have canceled for a variety of reasons. They could have had financial problems at the time. They might not have been satisfied with past service. They might have hired a competitor with a lower price, or maybe they did not offer a reason at all.

Whatever the case is, you always want to circle back with them because their circumstances might have changed. A lot of the clients I consult with are reluctant to call their past cancels. I often ask why. They certainly won't bite you if you call them, and many times they don't even remember why they canceled your service. It could have been something as simple as a small mistake you made and they overreacted emotionally and canceled. It may be that their feelings have changed. Sometimes, they leave over price, and a lot of times the lower-cost provider they are currently using is not meeting their needs in the way they expected.

Even if you don't reacquire these people as clients, you are showing them that you care, and you are leaving them with a good taste in their mouth. At the very least, you are gathering valuable information about why they left your service and making a note of it in your database. When I acquire other companies' lists, I am interested in the volume of canceled clients they have. These are easy new sales for our company once we have the information. Just think about it.: these prospects are proven consumers of lawn care and home services. Jackpot!

New Homeowners

This is another great list that can be purchased monthly or quarterly from a marketing company. This information comes from mortgage companies or telephone companies, as people need both loans and phones when they buy a new home. Again, when you upload this information into your calling software, you can program it to provide a list of existing clients your company has in close proximity to the new homeowner. This creates that familiarity and a warmer introduction. Additionally, new homeowners usually have a checklist of all of the services and utilities they need to hire or turn on. This can be an overwhelming experience, especially for those who have never owned a home before. If you call these folks right when they move in, you will be a lifesaver for them.

Besides that, your initiative and timeliness will help beat your competitors, as most homeowners will not have hired most of their service providers at that point. You will beat your competition to the punch. When this occurs, your sales call will be subjected to less price haggling, as the new homeowners will be motivated to get their new investment in tip-top shape. You can also time these calls to follow a direct mail campaign so that the new homeowners will have already received literature about your company when the call is made. This will make your introduction that much easier.

GAVE ESTIMATES

When you are aggressive in generating large volumes of sales, you will also find that you create large volumes of prospects who reject your offer. Not to worry. If you properly track these folks, they will turn into valuable data for you because you have already done the heavy lifting by simply connecting with them, educating them on your service, and providing them with pricing. When prospects reject your offer, you should mark this down in your software with a label such as "no to sale" or "gave estimate." Circling back to these prospects a few weeks or months later is a good idea, and when you call them again, it's an effortless and short pitch.

You may want to say, "Hi, Mrs. Smith, this is _____ from _____. The reason for my call is that we spoke a while back and you expressed some interest in our service. Just checking in to see if you would like to schedule that today?" As you can see, pitching "gave estimates" is short, sweet, and to the point. Just because the prospects did not buy when you originally pitched them does not mean they will not buy later. You may have called on these particular clients and made a great sales presentation, but still they declined your offer. Even more frustrating is when prospects call your company inquiring about your service, and you sell all of the benefits of your service, review service, and pricing options but still can't close the sale.

There are various reasons why prospects won't buy when it's time to close, but the reality is that it happens. As I tell my sales team, never burn that bridge. Gather all of the information you can on those prospects and save it in your database. Make a note that you gave an estimate and be specific about why the prospects did not close. Weeks, months, and even years later you can upload all of these "gave estimate" prospects into your predictive dialer and call them as a campaign. These are some of the warmest leads that you can contact, and they have already been pitched, so once you have them on the phone, you need waste little time and can go directly into trying to close them. Statistically, they have a much higher close rate, because rapport with them has already been built, and many times they feel they at least owe you an explanation as to why they did not buy from you in the past.

CALLBACKS

Callbacks, as we refer to them at our company, are prospects who listen to your sales pitch and express sincere interest but, for whatever reason, are not prepared to commit to your service at the time of your cold-call and ask you to call back at a later date. I have mixed feelings about this type of lead, because it is my feeling that if these prospects really wanted to buy from you, they would have done so at the time of your initial sales presentation. I think it takes a certain talent and ability to separate these prospects into two categories so that you preserve and protect your valuable time on the phone. The two categories are (1) those who genuinely are interested and qualified to buy from you, and (2) those who are simply too nice to say no.

It takes experience and skill to put your trust in people who request that you call them back at a later time. Personally, I am very selective when agreeing to callbacks. One might think that sounds ludicrous because, after all, the prospect appears to be someone who is interested in buying your service and thus should be considered a "lead." But in residential phone sales, people are not always honest with you, and you need to be good at weeding them out. That is why, when I have leads on the phone who request to be called at a later time, I always push as much as I can for them to buy right then and there.

In most cases, I simply read this type of request as a polite no. If prospects appear genuinely interested in buying my service but have time constraints at the time of my call, or if they legitimately need to check with their spouse or check the terms of a service contract they have with another company, I will grant them a callback. But this is only after they have made a very convincing case to me. When granting callback requests, it is important that you already have provided the prospects with adequate detail about the service you are selling, the terms, and the cost. I also recommend trial-closing them when you set up an exact time and date to call them again.

To do this, you could say something along the lines of "Okay, Mrs. Smith, so when I call you back on Friday, March 10, at 6 p.m., you plan on scheduling with me then, correct?" Typically, when you use this method of trial-closing, you will get a fairly good read on whether or not these prospects are serious about buying. If they begin to backpedal and stammer when they reply, you will know they are most likely just trying to get you off the phone. I think many people have a hard time saying no because they legitimately don't want to disappoint or let others down by rejecting them.

However nice they may think they are being, these prospects build up a false sense of hope for a salesperson, which is one of the cruelest things a prospect can do. This is even more the case when the prospect strings a sales rep along for days and even weeks with a series of requested callbacks. Callbacks create hope, and sales reps feed on that, anticipating the closing of these sales. When this occurs and the prospects finally reject the offer or make themselves unavailable to the sales rep by not answering the phone, it can be a crushing defeat for the sales rep. The dangerous aspect of these empty callbacks is not so much the loss of a potential sale for the sales rep but that it can so deflate and discourage even the most experienced rep that it can ruin an otherwise good sales day. Nothing can put sales reps into a dry funk as much as one of these rejections.

That is why I have created stringent rules in my company regarding this type of lead. Years ago I created the rule of four and no more for my sales team. This means a sales rep can make a total of four attempts to connect with a prospect who has requested a callback. The rep is allowed to make three more attempts after the first contact to connect and close the sale. After the fourth call, even if the rep has not actually spoken to the prospect, that rep is required to resolve the lead in the sales software and move on. As I always say to my sales reps who are being strung along by a callback prospect, "She's just not that into you. Move on, buddy. There are plenty of fish in the sea."

Although I joke about this topic, it really is something that is important to address. When you build up a bunch of these "empty leads" in your call log, you are just kidding yourself and creating a false sense of hope. You spend all of that time chasing down these leads, which are proven to be no more likely to buy than any new prospect you cold-call. I advocate putting your efforts into staying focused on the predictive dialer so that you maintain a positive mental attitude and keep moving forward, avoiding setbacks and distractions.

CHAPTER SEVEN

THE POWER OF CROSS-SELLING

Earlier in this book I highlighted the benefit of cross-selling new customers at the time of the sale. Many times, clients who have just been sold do not feel comfortable buying additional services immediately after they hire you. They need a few months to assess the level and quality of service your company delivers to them before they buy additional services from you. They need time to build trust. For example, some of my new clients will initially purchase a basic lawn care program, see the results and benefits of the service over the course of three or four months, and then express interest in buying a lawn aeration service or a tree and shrub care program. They make these decisions once we have built trust with them. Your active database is one of your biggest assets, and if you aren't marketing and cross-selling to these clients, you are missing out on hundreds of thousands of dollars in lost revenue per year. I strongly recommend regularly marketing to your active database of customers through email, direct mail, and up-sell inserts when you are mailing any literature out. You could mail them out each month with invoices, for example.

In my experience, you need to be in front of your customers and communicating with them every month about the benefits of the additional services you offer. Sometimes, this still isn't enough. The most effective tool for up-selling and cross-selling your clients is the telephone coupled with your own sales skills. There is nothing more frustrating than when one of my existing clients buys a service from a competitor, a service that I too offer. When this occurs, I blame no one but myself. The consumer views what we do a lot differently than we business owners do. For example, we might assume our clients know that we offer tree and shrub care at our lawn care company. But average consumers, especially the ones who are new to buying a certain service, are ignorant of the ins and outs of our industry.

It is up to us to clearly communicate to them what services we offer and don't offer. Although the other marketing efforts are great, and they create awareness, it doesn't mean that they close additional sales in your existing customer base. In order to take complete control over this, you need to build an effective in-house sales campaign and simply pick up the telephone and call your clients. You need to talk to them and highlight the benefits of your company's other services. When making these calls, you want to introduce yourself to your clients and let them know that you are making them aware of the other services your company offers, services that your clients may benefit from.

When you contact existing clients to let them know you are "checking in" with them or expressing concern over an issue they may have, you are truly disarming them. They will let their guard down in a way they wouldn't if you were simply calling to sell something. Once you put them at ease with your call in this way, they are more likely to listen to whatever else it is that you have to say. You can highlight other services or products you sell and your clients will remain receptive because you are not calling them just to sell something. When you use this approach, you add value, and your sales call comes across more powerfully.

CONCLUSION

This book is a collection of my thoughts, ideas, and strategies to help grow your business. I believe that success is only useful if shared. By sharing the art of teleselling, I hope that you will put into practice the insider tips I've designed for sales departments everywhere. These proven techniques are what I used to grow my brother's business into the success it is today, and they can do the same for your organization.

My One-Step Sales approach has been engineered for success from the very beginning. Throughout this book I introduced you to some difficult situations you and your team will encounter on the phone, provided some very pointed advice on how to avoid pitfalls, and shared with you my personal stories and experiences along the way. In return, I want nothing more than growth and prosperity for your business, and I want you to be able to develop a value proposition for your team and enhance your workplace. I hope you will refer to this book throughout your professional career and come back to it every now and again with new eyes.

From trial-closings to cross-selling to developing your specific and unique data universe, we have explored all areas that are important and necessary for every teleselling sales department. These aspects are nothing by themselves but everything when tied together. My One-Step Sales approach is a great tool that I hope you will learn from and implement in your business.

Printed in the USA
CPSIA information can be obtained
at www.ICGtesting.com
JSHW012052140824
68134JS00035B/3400